JOURNALISM

JOURNALISM

THE
ESSENTIALS
OF
WRITING
AND
REPORTING

JAMES MORRISON

ROBERT HALE

First published in 2015 by Robert Hale, an imprint of
The Crowood Press Ltd, Ramsbury, Marlborough Wiltshire SN8 2HR

www.crowood.com

This impression 2019

British Library Cataloguing-in-Publication Data
A catalogue record for this book is available from the British Library.

ISBN 978 0 7198 0985 9

Printed and bound in India by Replika Press Pvt. Ltd.

CONTENTS

PREFACE   9
The Structure of This Book

INTRODUCTION   13
The Origins of Journalistic Prose

ACKNOWLEDGEMENTS   16

PART I: GUIDE

1. The News Story   23
The News Story in Outline: The Role and Purpose of the 'Inverted
    Triangle' Structure
News in a Nutshell: The Art of the Twenty-Five-Word 'Intro'
People First
The First Three-par 'News-break'
Dropped Intros
News Language: Brevity, Clarity and Plain English

2. The Feature   43
Issue-based Features and News Backgrounders
Structuring Issue-based Features – Some General Conventions
Small is Beautiful
Packing a Punch
The 'Circular' Feature: From Beginning to Middle, and How to End it
Doing the Introductions: Interview-based Features
'Write-through' Interviews
Q&As – and When (and When Not) to Use Them
From 'How-to' to 'Tried-and-tested' – A Brief Word on Some
    Common Consumer Features

3   **Profiles and Obituaries**   65
    Showing Not Telling: Framing Your Character Sketch
    Casting Your Profile: The Opening Gambit
    Getting to Know You: The Case for Chronologically Driven Profiles
    Thematic Profiles
    Knowing Me, Knowing You: The First-person Perspective
    Profiling 'Things', Not People
    Profiling the Dead: Writing Obituaries
    Avoiding Hagiography
    Beware the 'Hatchet Job'

4   **Reportage**   82
    Reportage and 'Literary' Journalism
    From Riis to Capote: Investigative Reportage, Eyewitness Narratives
        and the 'Story-tellers'
    From 'Gonzo' to 'New' Journalism – The Evolution of Reportage,
        American-style
    Crusading Reportage

5   **The Journalistic Essay**   95
    The Rise of the 'Essayists' and their Place in Popular Journalism
    Essays for Specialist Audiences

6   **The Opinionated Journalist**   103
    The Art of Critical Reviewing
    'Sandwiches', 'Burgers' and the Art of Saying Just Enough – But Not
        Too Much
    The Top Half of the 'Bun' by Example – Some Common Ingredients
    Filling in the Gaps: The 'Meat' of the Article
    Cutting to the Chase – The Bottom Half of the Bun
    Meet the 'Opinion-formers': The Role of Op-ed Pieces and Leader
        Columns
    Stating Your Case without Sermonizing: The Art of the Leader
    Newspapers as 'Views-papers'
    Comment-based Blogs

7   **Journalism on the Go: From Live Tweeting to Online
    Content-writing**   126
    Live Blogging and Tweeting
    Multi-dimensional Multimedia Story-telling
    Crowd-sourced and Collaborative Investigative Reporting
    A Few Words about Content-writing

PART II: AID

8 Active versus Passive Writing   149
Verbs versus Adverbs – and When (and When Not) to Use Adjectives
Structuring Sentences and Prioritizing Information
Paragraphing and Signposting

9 Writing Visually   168
The Use of Filmic Imagery

10 Limiting the First Person   173
Trying Things out – Other Justifications for the First Person
How to 'Get Personal' while Avoiding 'I' and 'me'

11 Other General Issues in Journalistic Writing   180
Short versus Long Sentences: Striking the Right Balance
'Drip-feeding' Information: The Art of Teasing the Reader
Past versus Present Tense – and When to Use 'Which'
Direct Quotes versus Reported Speech
A Brief Warning about Clichés (and Puns)
Humour – and When and How to Use it
'Don't Use Semi-colons!' The Perils of the Extended Pause
House Style

12 The Editing Process   203
Time and Space: Editing to Length/Word Count
The Nuances of Cutting (against the Clock) – Shaving versus
   'Slash-and-burn'
Proofreading and Basic Sub-editing for Grammar, Spelling and Style

Afterword   209

Bibliography   215

Index of Names   217

General Index   221

PREFACE

'Journalism is literature in a hurry.' – Matthew Arnold

A COMMON CRITICISM OF written journalism is that it is clichéd, clumsily worded and colourless. While novelists, dramatists and poets agonize over every nuance of form and structure, so the argument goes, reporters and feature-writers are little more than jobbing hacks – thrashing out poorly researched news stories and 'think pieces' devoid of style, substance or even much in the way of thought to impossibly tight deadlines dictated by the crude commercial demands of their publishers. But while there is certainly some truth to accusations that many day-to-day articles for newspapers, magazines and online media are superficial and lacking in obvious 'literary' merit, it would be wrong to dismiss all (or even most) journalistic writing as inelegant and ephemeral. In fact, modern journalism is the product of a proud, ever-evolving tradition which has its origins as much in classical prose as the biting polemics of early pamphleteers. Moreover, journalism has counted among its practitioners some of our finest stylists and storytellers. In the English-speaking world alone, the trade has produced giants like Dickens, Orwell, Hemingway, Greene, Wodehouse and Chesterton – authors now so revered that we scarcely need bother to cite their first names. More recent examples of journalists-turned-authors include: Will Self (a prolific comment-writer for papers including

9

The Times, Guardian and *Independent*); Tom Wolfe (author of the hugely influential *New Journalism* and also critically acclaimed bestselling novels like *The Bonfire of the Vanities*); Martin Amis (a former literary editor of the *New Statesman*); and, of course, a long succession of 'Gonzo' journalists whose most celebrated work confidently straddled the (often porous) divide between fiction and first-person reportage – most notably Jack Kerouac (*On the Road*), Hunter S. Thompson (*Fear and Loathing in Las Vegas*) and Ken Kesey (*One Flew over the Cuckoo's Nest*).

This book is written by a journalist who would not presume to count himself among such illustrious company. I have, though, written professionally for much of the past twenty years – and for a wide variety of publications, ranging from British national newspapers (the *Daily Mail*, the *Independent on Sunday, The Times, The Guardian,* the *Daily Telegraph*) to niche consumer and trade magazines (the *Times Educational Supplement, History Today, The Ecologist,* the *Art Newspaper, Museums Journal* and others). My years as a full-time news reporter followed what was, until recently, the 'classic' trainee route for those embarking on journalistic careers from a standing start – i.e. without the advantage of family or 'old school tie' connections. I began on a sleepy little local weekly paper (the *North Devon Journal*) before progressing through, in turn, provincial dailies (the *Evening Herald*, Plymouth, and *The Argus*, Brighton) and a news agency (the Press Association) to the hallowed terrain known – by that point nostalgically, rather than with any regard to geographical accuracy – as 'Fleet Street'. During this protracted odyssey my output has included news stories, in-depth features, profiles, reviews, opinion pieces, academic articles, conference papers and, latterly, books. In addition, since 2003 I have taught journalism on a succession of professional practice courses at further and higher education institutions including City University, Kingston University and Goldsmiths, University of London.

The Structure of This Book

I am, then, someone who can claim to have written (and, perhaps more importantly, read) more than my fair share of journalism. And it is the eye for a vivid image, punchy intro and neat turn of phrase gained through this experience that I hope to demonstrate, above all, in this book. As with other titles in this series, my intention is twofold – and, to this end, it seems logical to divide the book into two distinct 'parts'. The first of these is concerned with introducing aspiring and 'early-career' journalists to the main forms and formats contemporary journalism takes. I begin by looking at what remains (even in this increasingly fluid 'multimedia' age) perhaps the most rigidly defined and structured journalistic article, the news story, before examining the more varied ways in which other familiar article types, such as features, profiles, reviews and comment pieces, are composed in print and online. As well as setting out the conventions underpinning these mainstays of written journalism I will, of course, illustrate them by quoting extracts from published articles by noted practitioners.

In the second part of the book I turn my attention to exploring more nuanced aspects of journalistic writing, and dispensing what might broadly be described as 'advice' for more experienced and developing journalists. These will include the importance of using active verbs and sentences; 'showing, not telling' stories; and, wherever possible, avoiding describing events and places by falling back on the lazy default option of which I am guilty here: using the first person. As has often been said, however, journalism is an inexact science – and in this brave new digital era of Facebook, Twitter and collaborative blogs, this truism is truer than ever. For this reason, I aim to be less prescriptive than provocative in the pointers I give – encouraging readers to be inventive, experimental and self-reflective and, above all, to read as widely as possible as they seek to make themselves better writers.

Finally, it would seem a good idea to close this preface by outlining a little more precisely what this book hopes to achieve. As ever, this is a question of defining it, at least partly, by what it is *not*. This is not, then, a book about what does (and does not) constitute subject matter deserving of journalistic attention. Neither is it about the process of 'getting' stories, snagging interviews or developing feature ideas – by, for instance, wading through documents, attending 'newsworthy' events and mining contacts for quotable reactions and opinions. All this, and much more besides, has already been extensively covered in any number of 'how-to' guides to 'being' a reporter or journalist. Equally, this does not pretend to be a guide to good English grammar: while one would hope the examples of journalistic writing it highlights do not commit any obvious 'offences' in terms of basic punctuation or spelling, in most cases I have chosen them to highlight examples of style, flair and effective story-telling, rather than dry technical precision. What you *should* gain from this book, however, is less an objective definition of what constitutes 'good' reporting – or even 'good' written journalism *in the round* – than an exploration of the various different forms that writing can take, backed by an appreciation of the 'tricks of the trade' the best practitioners use to inject life and meaning into their work.

INTRODUCTION

The Origins of Journalistic Prose

'JOURNALISM', WROTE THE LATE, sometimes great, always uncompromising literary critic Cyril Connolly, is one of the great 'enemies of promise' – a wasted effort; a diversion from, even a barrier to, true literary accomplishment. Where real literature could boast of 'texture' and 'formal and compact ... not immediately striking' qualities that repaid a second reading, the pressure on journalists to achieve their full 'impact' on the first left their prose necessarily 'loose, intimate, simple and striking' and, as a consequence, devoid of permanence. 'A journalist', he wrote, must 'accept the fact that his work, by its very today-ness, is excluded from any share in tomorrow'. Yet, as I hope this book demonstrates, journalistic writing in fact has a long and noble tradition – and one which has many more strings to its bow (to indulge in another Connolly pet hate, cliché) than he might have us believe.

As with so many historical developments, it is a moot point as to precisely how far back we can date the emergence of the first written journalism. A commonly held view is that journalism as most of us understand it – a mix of the reporting of events unlikely to come to light if it were left to the powers-that-be to tell us about them and invective aimed at those same establishment forces – only began in earnest with the grassroots pamphleteering fostered by the tempestuous political climate of seventeenth-century Europe. However, what might loosely be described as 'reporting' of *official* events and information arguably started at a much earlier stage, not least as a means used by the wealthy to share commercially useful intelligence and a tool for the powerful to spread propaganda. Thus, as early as the dawn of the fifteenth century, Italian and German merchants were circulating their own hand-written reports of significant political and economic developments among themselves in an effort to promote their collective business interests. Indeed, it is possible to view these highly exclusive, near-masonic channels of communication as an embryonic form of the more democratized, participative citizen journalism and networking via online social media which have become so integral to the dissemination of news and information in our own digital age.

But for every attempt to spread the word about important deeds and events (however narrowly or widely), there were equal and opposite efforts to suppress it. Britain's first semi-professional periodical, *A Current of General News*, was actually published as early as 1622, but it wasn't until the formal abolition of state censorship with the final repeal of the Licensing Act in 1694 that emerging papers and journals truly began to find their voice. Even as late as 1771 a printer named Miller was ordered by the Lord Mayor of London to cease publishing his illicit reports of debates in the UK Parliament – reliable records of which had to wait a further twenty-eight years to appear, courtesy of the similarly 'unlicensed' Thomas 'T.C.' Hansard. His daily entries in William Cobbett's radical *Political Register* would eventually lend their name to the official version of its proceedings.

It was through the radical writings of early crusaders for social reform, however, that journalistic prose really began to come of age in the post-censorship era. By the 1800s, the largely anonymous polemics by seventeenth-century agitators had given way to the more assertive, openly authored output of early campaigning journalists from equally humble roots, such as Thomas Paine (corset-maker-turned-author of the hugely influential constitutional tract, *Rights of Man*) and the aforementioned Cobbett (son of a farmer and publican). At the same time, the middle classes, too, were producing a generation of increasingly independent-minded editors and essayists, many of whom would earn fame as much for their fictional achievements as their journalism. These 'establishment' satirists and commentators – forerunners, in their way, of the Ian Hislops of today – included Henry Fielding, author of *Tom Jones* and co-founder of London's prototype police force, the Bow Street Runners; Jonathan Swift, a pamphleteer for first Tories, then Whigs, who went on to pen the allegorical *Gulliver's Travels*; and Daniel Defoe, writer of *Robinson Crusoe*, the first English novel.

But what of bona fide magazines and newspapers? And to what point can we date the origins of modern journalistic reporting, with its lofty pretensions towards balance and impartiality? In Britain, the first semi-professional paper to speak of was arguably the *Oxford Gazette* (later renamed the *London Gazette*), which first appeared in 1665. Yet, with censorship still alive and well at that time, much of what passed for the 'news' it carried about noteworthy people and events was prone to bowdlerization and hagiography – making it less a 'first draft of history' than an early form of the kind of dumbed-down rhetoric and PR-speak that continues to typify the weakest reporting on the rich and powerful to this day. By the time Samuel Buckley's *Daily Courant* entered print as Britain's first daily newspaper in 1702, the shackles had broken, and print journalism entered its first golden age, with the emergence of a wide range of well-informed, literate quarterly and monthly magazines – many of which survive. These included *The Tatler* – a source, then as now, of both highbrow news and febrile political gossip for the coffee-house-frequenting chattering classes – and, from 1785, the *Daily Universal Register*, which within three short years would change its name to *The Times*. While titles such as these were aimed squarely at educated audiences, the same licence to free speech that allowed them to gently mock and criticize the governing classes was soon being harnessed (invariably more brutally) to inform the 'masses' through emerging regional papers like the *North Briton* – the mouthpiece of radical pioneer John Wilkes.

By the close of the eighteenth century, then, the leisured and literary classes had their coffee-table reads and the stage was set for the rollout of not only a metropolitan press but also a regional (and, in due course, national) one – with newspapers increasingly acting as both engines and mirrors of democratic reform, on a mission to educate, empower and (of course) entertain the working classes. And, just as a British and European popular press with a newly inquisitive and questioning eye arose in parallel with the emergence of trades unions and campaigns to improve workers' rights and extend the voting franchise, nineteenth-century America saw the birth of what might be described as the first true 'investigative' journalism. By the time early news magnate Joseph Pulitzer purchased first the *St Louis Dispatch* and *St Louis Post* in 1879, then the *New York World* in 1882, written journalism on both sides of the Atlantic seemed remarkably spry. It is a testament to this then-emerging 'golden age' of popular journalism that the mix of human-interest stories, hard-hitting anti-corruption exposés, more in-depth features and occasional flashes of cheap sensationalism that Pulitzer and his contemporaries made their own has continued to serve the industry remarkably well into the twenty-first century.

Acknowledgements

THE AUTHOR AND PUBLISHER wish to thank the following individuals and organizations for permission to reproduce the following extracts:

'Michael Jackson is dead at 50', Nikki Barr, *Daily Express*, © Daily Express Syndication 2009
'Ramsay is "gagged" after row', Darren McCaffrey, *Daily Express*, © Daily Express Syndication 2009
'End of hated wind farms that ruin our countryside amid growing backlash over green energy', Macer Hall, *Daily Express*, © Daily Express Syndication 2013
'CD review: "Bowie – The Next Day"', Stephen Unwin, *Daily Express*, © Daily Express Syndication 2013
'Exclusive: Why Mrs Brown is as Feisty as Ever in D'Movie', Kirsty McCormack, *Daily Express*, © Daily Express Syndication 2014

Essential English for Journalists, Editors and Writers by Harold Evans and Crawford Gillan, published by Pimlico, reprinted by permission of The Random House Group Ltd

'Michael Jackson, King of Pop, dies of cardiac arrest in Los Angeles', Matthew Moore, *Daily Telegraph,* © Daily Telegraph Syndication 2009
'John Lydon interview', Andrew Perry, *Daily Telegraph,* © Daily Telegraph Syndication 2009
'Ian McEwan: Profile', Jake Kerridge, *Daily Telegraph,* © Daily Telegraph Syndication 2010
'Obituary: Sir Jimmy Savile', *Daily Telegraph,* © Daily Telegraph Syndication 2011
'Never Let Me Go, review', Tim Robey, *Daily Telegraph,* © Daily Telegraph Syndication 2011

'Tory MPs were paid to plant questions says Harrods chief', David Hencke, *The Guardian,* © The Guardian 1994
'Stars in their eyes (part one)', Jon Ronson, *The Guardian,* © The Guardian 2001
'Margaret Thatcher left a dark legacy that has still not disappeared', Hugo Young, *The Guardian,* © The Guardian 2003
'Suddenly the Iraq war is very real', Suzanne Goldenberg, *The Guardian,* © The Guardian 2003
'The moral agent', Giles Foden, *The Guardian,* © The Guardian 2007
'Interviewing Lou Reed: not a perfect day', Simon Hattenstone, *The Guardian,* © The Guardian 2003
'General election 2010: the liberal moment has come', *The Guardian,* © The Guardian 2010
'Stephanie Flanders: I'm the black sheep of my family', Andrew Anthony, *The Guardian,* © The Guardian 2011
'Confessions of the hack trade', Anthony Burgess, *The Guardian,* © The Guardian 2012
'Will the housing benefit cap cause the 'social cleansing' of London?', Polly Curtis, *The Guardian,* © The Guardian 2012
10 things not to say to someone when they're ill', Deborah Orr, *The Guardian,* © The Guardian 2012
'Residents to get more say over wind farms', Fiona Harvey, Peter Walker and agencies, *The Guardian,* © The Guardian 2013
'David Bowie: The Next Day – review', Alex Petridis, *The Guardian,* © The Guardian 2013
'Are iPads and tablets bad for young children?', Paula Cocozza, *The Guardian,* © The Guardian 2014

'Climate change efforts undermined', PA Mediapoint Newswire, 13 February 2014

'Ant and Dec join the great and good in Who's Who', *Daily Mail,* © Associated Newspapers 2009
'Vote DECISIVELY to stop Britain walking blindly into disaster', *Daily Mail,* © Associated Newspapers 2010
'Obsessive secrecy, a £30m fortune and the trauma that drove Kate Bush into hiding', Alison Boshoff, *Daily Mail,* © Associated Newspapers 2012
'Immigration a mistake? Come off it, Jack Straw!', Richard Littlejohn, *Daily Mail* © Associated Newspapers 2013

'Crime and Education', Charles Dickens, *Daily News*, September 1843

'What is poverty?', A. C. Grayling, *Prospect,* © Prospect Magazine Limited, from a Prospect report on poverty, 2013

'Never Let Me Go', Tom Huddlestone, *Time Out*, 8 February 2011

'McBride spinning for his career', Guido Fawkes, www.Order-Order.com, 11 April 2009, © www.Order-Order.com.

'British scientist blames James Bond villain for unpopularity of nuclear power', Justin McKeating, www.greenpeace.org, 12 January 2012, © www. greenpeace org.

'Sikhs v Muslims: why the debate on grooming isn't about the women themselves', Sunny Hundal at www.liberalconspiracy.org, © www.liberalconspiracy.org 2007–2013

George Orwell, *The Lion and the Unicorn: Socialism and the English Genius,* © George Orwell, 1941. Reprinted with permission of Bill Hamilton as the Literary Executor of the estate of the late Sonia Brownell Orwell.
George Orwell 'Politics and the English Language', Penguin Classics, 2013

'Something's wrong', Melanie McGrath, *Tate* magazine, © Tate Magazine, London 2002

'The Full Monty', www.whatsonstage.com, Michael Coveney 2014, © 1999–2014 WhatsOnStage.com,Inc

How to be a Woman, Caitlin Moran, published by Ebury, 2012. Reprinted with permission of The Random House Group Ltd.

'Justice at Night', Martha Gellhorn, *The Spectator,* 20 August 1936, © 2015 The Spectator (1828) Ltd

Andy Beckett, *When the Lights Went Out*, Faber and Faber, 2009

Jonathan Freedland, *Bring Home the Revolution: The Case for a British Republic,* Fourth Estate, 1998. Reprinted by permission of HarperCollins Publishers Ltd, © Jonathan Freedland (1998)

John Harris, *The Last Party*, Fourth Estate, 2003. Reprinted by permission of HarperCollins Publishers Ltd, © John Harris (2003)

Cole Moreton, *Hungry for Home*, published by Viking, 2000

Hunter S. Thompson, *Hell's Angels: A Strange and Terrible Saga*, Penguin Books Ltd, 1999, © Hunter S. Thompson (1999)

PART I: GUIDE

1. THE NEWS STORY

BY DEFINITION, NEWS STORIES are preoccupied with the 'new'. Whereas other types of journalistic article might focus on themes or issues of wider topical interest, adopting a more discursive and/or analytical approach to exploring their background and context, the immediate reporting of newsworthy events and incidents is necessarily concerned with sketching in the 'who, what, where, when, how, why' elements of something 'newsworthy' – and doing so as soon as possible after it has occurred (if not beforehand). Moreover, in this multimedia age of endlessly rolling, 24/7 news headlines, there is little that remains new for long. Rather, there is an increasing expectation among news 'audiences' (you and me) that we will be able to access written, broadcast and/or multimedia reports of newsworthy happenings almost as soon as they take place. In the case of major 'breaking' stories like train crashes, elections, wars or natural disasters, we may even expect to find out what is happening *while* the 'events' are still in the process of unfolding.

Given the lengthy (and costly) production routines involved in writing, laying out and printing physical newspapers, today's primary medium for this minute-by-minute rollout of written news content is online. In the fast-evolving twenty-first-century media environment, the latest news is relayed less by the evening or early-morning print editions of papers themselves than on their accompanying websites, on more specialist news sites and e-zines, or via 'ticker-tape-style' single-line updates beamed to our smartphones and tablet computers by RSS (Really Simple Syndication) feeds, blogs, or subscription-based news services. It is now not only possible but (for millions of news 'consumers') *routine* to be continually bleeped, buzzed or otherwise badgered by news 'alerts' focusing on everything from goal-by-goal Premiership football coverage to celebrity gossip. Moreover, the traditional gatekeeper role of *professional* journalists is increasingly being challenged (if not quite supplanted as yet) by emailed, tweeted or uploaded 'frontline dispatches' from eyewitnesses and those caught up in unfolding events. At their best, these so-called 'citizen journalists' supply first-hand accounts and authentic quotes which can greatly enrich the quality of published stories.

The News Story in Outline: The Role and Purpose of the 'Inverted Triangle' Structure

These, then, are the channels through which written news reports increasingly reach us. But what form and structure does latter-day news copy take? For stories to fulfil their *raison d'être* of being timely, thorough and to the point, they must be written in a punchy and precise style. And, given the plethora of outlets from which today's 'consumers' can access their news coverage, each reporter (and the publication for which he or she works) is under more pressure than ever to make his or her 'version' of a story stand out from the crowd – achieving the all-important paper sales figures and online hits/page impressions that attract advertisers in a highly competitive commercial market. Moreover, in this era of ever-longer working hours, and ever-more congested leisure time, news has to compete for our attention with numerous other distractions as we commute to and from jobs, juggle family and social commitments, and are all the while bombarded with a daily deluge of digital communications. All the more reason for stories to 'grab' our attention – and, having done so, to hold it.

Before plunging into the detail of how news stories are structured in print and on screen, it is worth giving very brief consideration to the question of how journalists decide what is (and isn't) news in the first place. As the preface makes clear, this is not a book about news values or news-gathering (there are already plenty of those). However, the day-to-day news 'instincts', or 'judgments', that determine what news organizations do and don't report – and, importantly, how much space they allocate to one story over another – is an important part of the writing process in one key respect. By choosing to report/highlight one event over another, editors and (to a lesser extent) reporters are involved in a process of both *selection* and *construction*. They are selective in that they choose to report only the events – births, deaths, marriages, speeches, court cases, crimes, policy announcements etc. – that they consider to be of potential interest to their readers. Effectively, this means that the 'editing' process (something we will be examining in detail only in the very last chapter of this book) begins long before individual reporters and writers are faced with the onerous task of cutting the lengths of their articles to the pre-decided word counts demanded by the slots allocated to them on the page. At the same time, journalists are engaged in a process of constructing our overall impressions of 'the news' on a given day, at a given time. In no small sense, then, they are involved in editing 'reality' itself – or choosing which *bits* of news to fish out for us from the pool of *potential* stories that 'objectively' exist and, having done so, deciding how to put together the facts they have chosen to inform us about on the page. As the journalist-cum-academic Walter Lippmann once memorably put it, journalists are responsible for nothing less than shaping the 'pictures in our heads'.

But in a more mundane, everyday sense, what 'form' do these news constructs take? For reasons detailed at length elsewhere, straightforward news reports in the Anglo-American media have long been presented in a highly structured form conventionally known as the 'inverted triangle' or 'inverted pyramid' (see Figure 1.1). The idea is that the main *gist* of the story should be outlined as swiftly and economically as possible, with its all-important 'who, what, where, when, how, why' elements – popularly, if somewhat erroneously, known as the 'five Ws' – sketched out in the space of a single introductory sentence, or *intro* Having hopefully ensnared readers by giving them the bare bones of the story, the reporter's next task is to draw them in further, by starting to put 'flesh' on those bones through the weaving-in of more detailed information about *precisely* who did what to whom, and *exactly* where and when the event in question took place. This they will need to do in the space of the next two sentences or paragraphs of the story – the second of which will often include a quotation from one of the main protagonists or someone else with the authority and/or knowledge to commentate on what has occurred. From this point on, the report will tend to be concerned less with the immediate 'facts' of the story itself than with the *reaction* to it from interested parties and relevant *background detail* that may be useful to help readers put the story into context. Assuming the article is structured correctly, the further down the copy the reader's eyes wander, the less vital and immediate should be the information they encounter. In all but a handful of exceptional story types (for instance, a report on a serious crime that culminates in a police appeal for witnesses or a story about an upcoming public event) the copy will effectively 'fizzle out', with its final sentences reserved for peripheral detail that, if necessary, could easily be cut from the published article by sub-editors without undermining its impact – or omitting anything readers need to know to fully understand it.

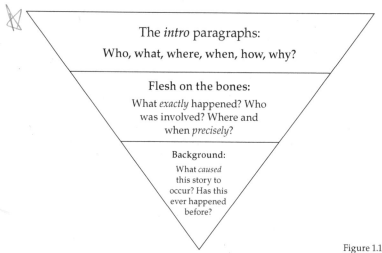

The *intro* paragraphs:
Who, what, where, when, how, why?

Flesh on the bones:
What *exactly* happened? Who was involved? Where and when *precisely*?

Background:
What *caused* this story to occur? Has this ever happened before?

Figure 1.1

News in a Nutshell: The Art of the Twenty-Five-Word 'Intro'

When writing a news article, then, it is important to outline the essence of the story as swiftly and economically as possible. This is especially the case in relation to so-called 'hard' news: stories focusing on serious, dramatic and/or controversial subject matter such as crimes, political events or gritty social issues. The urgency of getting across the 'five Ws' in a no-nonsense, succinct way that captures and holds the reader's attention has for many years seen reporters in the English-speaking world inculcated in the importance of summing up their stories in twenty-five words or fewer. Of course, in some forms of contemporary media news has now been reduced to such a bite-sized commodity that even this modest word count is considered generous. For instance, it is customary for the red bars used to flash up significant 'breaking news' developments as they happen on the BBC News Channel, Sky News or CNN – not to mention the (sometimes barely gram-matical) updates specialist news providers fire off to subscribing mobile-users – to be worded in a highly abbreviated, staccato style once reserved for headlines and captions. And this trend has been reflected in various other areas of media communica-tion of late. The musings of celebrities and politicians on social networking website Twitter are these days frequently quoted directly by journalists as the top lines of their stories – yet, five years after its launch, the maximum tweet remains a mere 140 characters in length.

Such 'new-fangled' developments aside, the conventional twenty-five-word news intro remains a staple of much of the news published to this day in print and online by the British and American provincial and national press. Indeed, the craft of encapsulating the main angle (or angles) of a story in these rela-tively few, well-chosen words is considered crucial to persuading people to begin reading it and, having done so, to continue until the end. The importance of journalistic sentences – particu-larly intros – being worded in an 'active' way will be explored in more detail in Chapter 8. Nevertheless, it is worth rehearsing here in the context of the need for news intros, in particular, to meet certain requirements in order to be effective. Primarily, they should strive to tell the reader something *concrete*: in other words that someone (or something) has done, or is going to do, something to (or about) someone or something else. To be more technical, an intro needs to respect one of the original basic 'rules' of English grammar, in that it should contain both a *subject* (the individual or organization doing the something) and an *object* (the thing – or, indeed, person – to which/whom something is being done). Beyond this, it should also strive to be exact. Vagueness has no place in such writing, and woe betide rookie reporters who file their copy with terms that fudge specific details. To editors, flaky terms like 'several', 'could', 'may be' or 'is expected to' smack of yawning gaps in their journalists' research, woolly thinking and attempts to gloss over the absence of crucial information they have failed to find out. Moreover, intros should never take it as read that the audience at which they are aimed is already conversant with all the background to a story – particularly when that background is a tangled and complex one. A story about the latest development in a long-running local planning saga, for instance (a staple of provincial papers everywhere), must avoid opening with an introductory paragraph that a new reader ignorant of the earlier twists and turns is incapable of understanding. Not for nothing have journalism trainers grown hoarse reminding their charges never to 'assume' anything about their readers – least of all prior knowledge.

To illustrate the importance of active, precise, self-explanatory intros – with their faithful 'five Ws' and subjects 'doing something' to objects – it is worth applying another key maxim to be explored in Chapter 8. The following examples have been chosen to *show*, rather than *tell*, how this end might be achieved. In the first instance, let us look at two different intros to the same story from British national newspapers at different points on what might be called the tabloid–broadsheet spectrum. The story in question was one of those rare events to achieve blanket coverage across the world's media, from red-top scandal sheets to in-depth current affairs programmes, within hours of becoming public: the sudden death of megastar singer Michael Jackson from an apparent heart attack on 25 June 2009. The first intro sample is taken from mid-market UK tabloid paper the *Daily Express* and the second from 'quality' broadsheet title the *Daily Telegraph*:

> KING of pop Michael Jackson died last night after suffering a heart attack at his home.
>
> (Nikki Barr, 'Michael Jackson is dead at 50', www.express.co.uk, 26 June 2009)

> Michael Jackson, the world's most famous and controversial pop star, has died at the age of 50 after suffering a cardiac arrest at his Los Angeles home.
>
> (Matthew Moore, 'Michael Jackson, King of Pop, dies of cardiac arrest in Los Angeles', www.telegraph.co.uk, 26 June 2009)

What most marks out the first from the second version of the same story is its succinctness: in just sixteen words, the *Express* reporter, Nikki Barr, manages to convey the 'who' (Jackson), 'what' (his death), 'where' (at his home), 'when' (last night) and 'how' (heart attack) aspects of the story, leaving readers in absolutely no doubt about what has transpired. And, though there could be few people reading this article who had never heard of the American icon, she nonetheless remembers the importance of keeping her whole audience with her as she relays the dramatic events – prefiguring the use of Jackson's name with the oft-applied epithet 'king of pop'. She does not manage (quite) to explain 'why' Jackson has died – in order to do so she would arguably have had to rely on pure conjecture, given that she was writing so soon after news of his death had broken, and with the inevitable inquest (a major undertaking, given the scale of his fame) not yet begun. Contrast the brevity of Barr's telling of the story with the more rambling (twenty-seven-word) intro to the *Telegraph* piece. Though it covers the bases reasonably effectively, it needlessly breaks up the intro with a sub-clause that has the effect of interrupting the flow of the sentence and substituting a punchy phrase like 'king of pop' with the drawn-out (and borderline tautological) description 'most famous and controversial'. Although there are very few people for whom this can be said, it is also arguable that everyone reading the article will already know who Jackson is: he is, or was, one of the handful of public figures who (by the time of his death) genuinely needed no introduction. While the inclusion of Jackson's relatively young age perhaps adds a further note of poignancy missing from the *Express* story, it necessitates lengthening this all-important nut-shell sentence by five words. The result is a sentence that feels overloaded with information which might easily have been woven in gradually as the story wound on (as happened in the *Express* case).

For all the merits of one version of this particular story over the other, though, neither can easily be accused of leaving its readers bemused about the significance or 'meaning' of the event reported. This is not always the case, however, and there are times when highly newsworthy and important stories lose impact on the page (printed or online) because of the tortuous phraseology used by journalists to convey them and/or the assumptions about prior knowledge implicit in their reporting. The following intro is taken from a celebrated 1990s front-page lead (or 'splash') by *Guardian* journalists investigating the simmering political scandal that came to be known as 'cash for questions' and ultimately led to two ministerial resignations, a public inquiry, major reform of the system by which British MPs and peers were required to register their outside interests, and at least two libel suits against the paper (both of which it won). It is intriguing to note how – despite the article's undoubted impact, as later recognized by *The Guardian*'s being named 'Newspaper of the Year' in the British Press Awards – it struggles to meet the standard in terms of immediate clarity:

A Westminster lobbying company was paid tens of thousands of pounds to give to two high-flying Conservative MPs
for asking parliamentary questions at £2,000 a time on behalf
of Harrods during the height of the Lonrho and House of
Fraser controversy.

(David Hencke, 'Tory MPs were paid to plant questions says
Harrods chief', *The Guardian*, 20 October 1994)

The intro starts well enough. It begins by sketching in the 'who' (Westminster lobbying firms and Tory MPs), 'what' (payment of five-figure sums for parliamentary favours) and 'where' (in Parliament), if not the 'when', 'how' and 'why' elements of the story, and wisely holds back the identities of the politicians involved (Neil Hamilton and Tim Smith) – neither of whom were household names at the time. However, it comes unstuck badly towards the end, by assuming a whole groundswell of background knowledge on the part of its readers about what turns out, much further down in the story, to be a highly technical commercial dispute between the two parties which are named, Lonrho and House of Fraser. In so doing, it runs the risk of committing two reporting heresies: distracting readers from the nub of the story (corrupt payments to elected representatives) and, worse still, turning them away by isolating anyone who is unfamiliar with the (in itself, rather dry) business wrangles that motivated the lobbying firm to try to buy influence. Much better, surely, to have ended the sentence with the words 'on behalf of Harrods owner Mohamed Al-Fayed' – who is the high-profile and flamboyant figure revealed (in the third paragraph) to be the source of not only the payments but the story itself.

Although much of this section has been preoccupied with the need for succinctness in news intros, it is possible to become *too* obsessed with striking out all but the simplest nouns and verbs. In their classic work *Essential English for Journalists, Editors and Writers* – still regarded as the definitive 'how-to' guide to journalistic language – former *Sunday Times* editor Harold Evans and his co-author, Crawford Gillan, warn that too 'staccato' a news style can leave reports 'colourless'. They illustrate this point by contrasting a short intro which is vivid, lively and contains all the key information with a lengthier version, which, despite containing eleven more words, somehow contrives to be *less* evocative and informative. These two imagined intros read as follows:

An American soldier dragged a refugee across the Berlin Wall yesterday. The East Germans were shooting all the time. The refugee was wounded but his life is not in danger.

An American military policeman braved a hail of bullets to pull a wounded refugee over the Berlin Wall yesterday.

(from *Essential English for Journalists, Editors and Writers* by Harold Evans and Crawford Gillan, published by Pimlico, reprinted by permission of The Random House Group Ltd)

The first of these intros breaks at least two cardinal rules of good journalistic English: it contains three sentences, rather than one, and needlessly mentions its 'object' (the refugee) twice. The second intro works so much better because it combines the key details from all three sentences into a single one that is far more active. We encounter the near-cinematic image of a 'hail of bullets' descending on the American rescuer, rather than being left to surmise that the upshot of the first and second sentences in intro one is that he was in danger for his own life because the East Germans were 'shooting all the time'. Crucially, in the second intro, the writer brings together these two dramatic elements – the American and the East Germans' bullets – and, in so doing, makes the intro not only more visual but more *meaningful*. The one detail left out of intro two is the fact that the rescued man, though 'wounded', is not dying. If we were minded to be harsh, we might criticize its writer for leaving out this fact. However, a counter-argument is that this detail could sit happily in the second paragraph. Indeed, the story-telling process as a whole arguably benefits from its being placed there, as the fact the man was wounded (but we do not yet know how badly) entices people to continue reading.

The task, then, is to strike a balance: to find a form of words that is as bright as it is tight. And cracking the 'art' of writing tight, bright news intros is invariably one of the trickiest challenges for trainee reporters, particularly those whose prior writing experience has been confined to traditional academic essays and/or penning the occasional poem or short story. Once you can do so, however, the rewards are considerable, as almost every aspect of reporting – not just the process of putting down your ideas 'on paper' – suddenly feels easier. The discipline of intro-writing is as much about crystallizing in your mind the precise angle of a news story (which is key to structuring the piece as a whole) as it is about expressing that angle crisply and exactly in a sentence of fewer than twenty-five words. Not for nothing is it often said that, once you have your intro, the rest of the story 'will write itself'. Indeed, in certain cases, writing the intro is pretty much all the journalist need worry about: the shortest form of story, the 'News In Brief' (NIB), is seldom much longer than a single paragraph, meaning that *all* the essential information readers need to make sense of it must be contained in forty or fifty words.

People First

Another vital element of the way journalists approach news-writing to make sure they are maximizing the impact of their intros is to always try to put 'people first'. If the purpose of journalism is to inform, educate and entertain audiences, to do so it needs to persuade them it is worth reading. As audiences are made up of people, it is self-evident that they are more likely to read an article if they can identify with what it is about – if not directly (i.e. by relating it to their own life experiences), then because it at least concerns *other people* with whom they can empathize. Intros, then, need to present a 'human face' in order to attract (and hold) readers. Stories are never really about *things*: they are all, in some way, about *people*, and this should be reflected in the whole way in which they are worded, structured and laid out on the page – from the top down. Take the following two contrasting intros about a subject that has become a bête noire for many of those living in rural areas and villages around the UK. It concerns the British government's decision to introduce new planning rules making it easier for local communities to block proposals by developers to build onshore 'wind farms' in their areas. The two intros – lifted from the *Daily Express* and *Guardian*, respectively – demonstrate how a dreary staple of local newspapers, the planning policy story, can be made to seem 'more distant from' or 'closer to' readers through an individual reporter's decision about how to frame it:

MINISTERS will call a halt today to the spread of wind farms across the countryside amid a growing public backlash over green energy.

(Macer Hall, 'End of hated wind farms that ruin our countryside amid growing backlash over green energy', www.express.co.uk, 6 June 2013)

Residents will be able to stop the construction of wind-farms [sic] under tough rules that could seriously restrict the growth of onshore wind power generation.

(Fiona Harvey, Peter Walker and agencies, 'Residents to get more say over windfarms', www.guardian.co.uk, 6 June 2013)

Perhaps unusually, of the two intros quoted here, it is *The Guardian*'s that 'humanizes' the story most effectively – in so doing, drumming home its relevance to many of the paper's readers. Despite its rather ugly conflation of the two words 'wind farms' and its laboured second-half wording, the intro goes straight in on the prospective impact of the new policy proposal on people (in this case, the 'residents' set to be empowered by the legislation). As all readers will be residents of somewhere – whether their own property or one they rent from someone else – the reporters have created an immediate point of identification to which most will be able to relate. By contrast, the *Express* reporter is guilty of one of the cardinal sins of journalism: going in not on 'real' people but on policy-makers ('ministers'), and making no direct reference to anyone you or I might relate to at all (bar the somewhat clichéd, and abstract, term 'public backlash'). At best, this approach may egg readers on for all the wrong reasons – luring them into speculating about what their despised government is up to now. At worst, it could act as a complete switch-off: deterring them from reading on at all and, in so doing, failing to inform them about a story that might be directly relevant to their lives.

If a story is not 'about' people in the first instance, it is the journalist's job to 'make' it so. This process has two stages. Firstly, the reporter should try to *project* the story forward through his or her research – by speaking to people affected by what is happening/about to happen (and who have an opinion on it) and using this 'human-interest' material to *move the angle on* from a mere statement of what is being done, launched or proposed. Secondly, they need to *go in on* these views/reactions when they commit their story to the page. Crucially, a story which might otherwise have been about *things being done to* a town, a country or its people becomes about those people *saying, arguing or doing something* in response to *it*.

Chapter 8 of this book will go into further detail about the importance of structuring individual sentences in the right order, in the context of its discussion of 'active' story-telling.

The First Three-Para 'News-Break'

If the job of the news intro is to 'grab' readers and give them the main gist of the story, it is the role of the next two paragraphs to both *hold* their interest and offer them a fuller understanding of *exactly* what has happened – and (on the frequent occasions when the first para doesn't quite achieve this) how and why it came to pass. To repeat an imperfect metaphor, the intro should provide the skeleton of the report, while the second and third paras need to put flesh on its bones. By the third para – or, at the very latest, fourth – it is also the convention that the reporter will have included the first direct quotation from a source. This is designed to have two important effects: to *humanize* the story, by allowing one of its key protagonists to describe or respond to it, and to *authenticate* it, by demonstrating, through the inclusion of an attributed quote, that it actually occurred. Before launching into a quote, however, the reporter must be mindful of the fact that – in order for the words within speech marks to make sense – the paras preceding the quote must have done sufficient 'work' between them to *set up* the story, by covering (and elaborating on) the hallowed 'five Ws'.

By returning to the Michael Jackson example cited previously, one can see how, with variable success, news reporters wrestle to meet the requirements placed on their supporting paragraphs. The second and third paras of the *Express*'s Jackson story read as follows:

> His brother, Jermaine Jackson, said he believed the 50-year-old singer suffered a cardiac arrest at his Holmby Hills home in Los Angeles yesterday and was taken to the UCLA medical centre where he was pronounced dead at 2.26pm. The self-styled king of pop was due to perform 50 farewell concerts in London this summer, bowing out on an illustrious music career spanning several decades while aiming to resurrect his fortunes.
>
> Jackson's brother told reporters: 'My brother, the legendary King of Pop, passed away on Thursday June 25 at 2.26pm.'
>
> (Nikki Barr, 'Michael Jackson is dead at 50', www.express.co.uk, 26 June 2009)

If there is one obvious flaw to the second para it is that its first sentence clearly breaches the customary 'twenty-five words or fewer' rule. Beyond this stylistic slip, though, is there anything intrinsically *missing* from the overall paragraph that we need in order to understand/appreciate the quote that follows? Given the stark nature of this particular story – Jackson's sudden death – there is arguably only so much we can expect this second para to add to our knowledge of what has happened and, indeed, a limit to what we can really expect in the early reaction from one of his closest relatives. On both these scores, the story delivers: the second para puts flesh on the intro's skeleton by telling us that 'the 50-year-old' ('who') is believed to have suffered a cardiac arrest ('what' and, to some extent, 'how') at his 'Holmby Hills home' in LA (exactly 'where') yesterday ('when'), before being 'pronounced dead' at the UCLA medical centre at precisely 2.26 p.m. (a further extension of the 'when' and 'where'). It goes on to qualify its initial 'king of pop' conceit by referring to it as a 'self-styled' term, while contextualizing the timing of the star's death by informing (or, in many cases, *reminding*) the reader of the irony that he had been due to perform fifty highly publicized 'farewell concerts' in London later that summer. The scene is then set for his brother Jermaine's pithy but emotive tribute.

The *Telegraph's* second and third paras, by contrast, read as follows:

> Jackson was rushed to UCLA Medical Centre in a coma but doctors were unable to revive him. He was just weeks away from beginning a fifty-date comeback tour in London.
>
> His unexpected death has devastated fans and sparked a flood of tributes from the biggest names in the music industry. It has also led to speculation as to what killed him.
>
> (Matthew Moore, 'Michael Jackson, King of Pop, dies of cardiac arrest in Los Angeles', www.telegraph.co.uk, 26 June 2009)

As can be seen, these supporting paras end without offering us a quote – and, in fact, it is not until the fifth that we first encounter quotation marks, in the form of a single-word 'teaser' quote from Jackson's lawyer, Brian Oxman, which begins the process of enlarging on the sinister undercurrent to the story hinted at towards the end of para three. That this latter element is introduced at all, however, arguably gives the *Telegraph's* 'first three-para break' a slight edge over the *Express's*, in terms of its overall narrative impact. Not only is the broadsheet's summation of the immediate chronology of the previous day's events punchier than the tabloid's – notably using the word 'coma' and describing the frantic efforts of doctors to revive the singer – but it also introduces what amounts to a second, even more dramatic, strand to the story. This is the suggestion that mystery surrounds the actual *cause* of Jackson's death – a question mark which deftly nudges us closer to addressing the elusive 'fifth W' of the story (namely the reason 'why' he suffered his fatal seizure in the first place). On this occasion, then, the prolonged delay before a full quotation is arguably worth the wait, as when it does come it offers us something more journalistically satisfying than the more predictable (if heartfelt) expressions of sadness by Jackson's family at news of his passing, as illustrated below:

> 'This is not something that has been unexpected ... because of the medications which Michael was under,' Mr Oxman told CNN. 'I do not know the extent of the medications that

he was taking but the reports we had been receiving in the
family is that they were extensive. When you warn people
that this is what's going to happen and then it happens ...
where there's smoke, there's fire.'

(Ibid.)

The fact remains, though, that – while the first three paras of the
Telegraph story do put flesh on the proverbial skeleton's bones
rather well – in delaying inclusion of the first quote they bend
the rules when it comes to humanizing and authenticating the
story near the top. This is one end that, crucially, *The Guardian*'s
'cash for questions' investigative story achieves:

> Neil Hamilton, now minister at the Department of Trade and
> Industry responsible for business probity, and Tim Smith,
> junior Northern Ireland minister, were both named yester-
> day as recipients of payments passed to Ian Greer Associates
> by Mohamed Al-Fayed, the owner of Harrods, on top of a
> £50,000 fee for a parliamentary lobbying campaign.
>
> Mr Al-Fayed said yesterday: 'I felt it was now my public
> duty to make these facts known.'

(David Hencke, *The Guardian*, 20 October 1994)

In this respect, if not in the diluted impact of its awkward intro,
the story achieves its goal of hooking the reader – or, at least,
any reader who has made the effort to persevere beyond its first
paragraph.

Some news organizations have turned covering the main
points in their opening three paragraphs into a fine art. This
is especially true of news-wire providers, such as Reuters and
the Press Association – whose *raison d'être* is to provide reporters elsewhere with the 'bare bones' of a breaking story, as they
scramble to upload their 'first takes' to their websites, while
juggling phone calls and/or knocking on doors in an effort to
obtain further details and quotes they can use to enhance it later
on. The classic rule of thumb for news-wire reporters is that, if
'struck off' the main body of their copy, their first three paras
will still read like a complete – if heavily truncated – story in

their own right. The following extract from a 13 February 2014 Press Association story about a row between Liberal Democrat and Conservative ministers in Britain's Coalition government offers a good example of the self-contained news-break:

> Government efforts to combat climate change are being deliberately undermined by elements of the Conservative Party, a Liberal Democrat Cabinet minister is claiming.
>
> Energy Secretary Ed Davey says attempts by some Tories – combined with the UK Independence Party – to discredit the scientific evidence of climate change threaten a break-down of the political consensus on the issue.
>
> In a speech to the Institute for Public Policy Research think-tank, he will accuse critics of Government policy of a 'wilfully ignorant, head in the sand, nimby-ist conservatism', ignoring the risks of a world in which extreme weather events were much more likely.
>
> ('Climate change efforts undermined', PA Mediapoint Newswire, 13 February 2014)

Although the intro arguably omits the 'where' element of the 'five Ws' (a detail for which we have to wait until the third para), all other key elements are present in a sentence of a mere twenty-three words. The second para fills in most of the necessary gaps – naming the Minister concerned and contextualizing his comments by referring to a wider 'political consensus' about the need to recognize, and address, climate change. Most crucially, the third para provides the all-important 'evidence' to back up the story's intro angle, by including a strongly worded quote from Mr Davey which leaves the reader (and, presumably, those at whom it is targeted) in no doubt about the precise nature of his criticism.

Dropped Intros

Though news intros are generally required to 'hit the ground running', there are times when stories benefit from a slower, more considered, style of opening. A device commonly used by journalists writing 'softer' and quirkier stories – generally those with a strong human-interest slant – is the dropped intro. This is a form of elongated intro which may stretch over as many as three or four paragraphs, with initial sentences acting as 'teasers' or 'scene-setters' and the last one providing the 'punchline'. The role of this punchline is to spell out the story's angle for anyone who has not yet worked it out for themselves, and if it fails to do so adequately the dropped intro cannot be considered to have worked.

Though reporters sometimes stand accused of using dropped intros to disguise the fact that a story lacks substance – by drawing readers in with a natty turn of phrase calculated to distract them from a lack of incident or depth – at best, they can greatly enhance the quality of news prose by injecting colour and description that is lacking in most 'straight' news-writing. There are two types of dropped intro, both of which draw on the more slow-burn prose style normally associated with features. These are the simple drop and the delayed drop. A good example of a simple drop – a one-para teaser followed by a punchline which clearly spells out the angle of the story – is this playful intro about foul-mouthed TV chef Gordon Ramsay from the pen of *Daily Express* reporter Darren McCaffrey:

> He is famed for his colourful language and frank views – most recently likening a talk show host to a pig.
>   But there was little danger of any outburst from Gordon Ramsay yesterday after he stuck his mouth up with masking tape.
>
> (Darren McCaffrey, 'Ramsay is "gagged" after row', *Daily Express*,
> 4 July 2009)

The British national newspaper perhaps most associated with dropped intros is the *Daily Mail*. Though it has a tendency to overuse them – often as a lazy default option for its numerous celebrity-oriented stories – at its best, it employs them with a brio and lightness of touch lacking in other titles. The following example is a textbook illustration of how a delayed drop can be used to tantalize the audience, before finally putting their minds to rest about the angle of a story:

> They have rarely been off our television screens for the past two decades.
> From child actors in the BBC drama Byker Grove, to presenters of prime time hits I'm A Celebrity ... Get Me Out Of Here, Britain's Got Talent and Saturday Night Takeaway, Ant and Dec have been pretty hard to avoid.
> Now the Geordie duo's achievements have been deemed considerable enough to gain them each an entry into the Who's Who book.
>
> ('Ant and Dec join the great and good in Who's Who',
> www.dailymail.co.uk, 7 December 2009)

Where this intro differs to the previous example is in the degree of leisure it takes to get to the point. While one of the initially hidden elements of the story (the identity of the celebrities to which it refers) is given away at the start of its second paragraph (and in the headline), we have to wait until the end of the third to find out *exactly* what the story is about. To this end, it delivers the requisite punch, by luring us in with titbits of information before finally hitting us between the eyes with a genuinely incongruous 'twist'.

For all the merits of dropped intros, though, like any other 'literary conceit' it is wise for journalists to use them sparingly. While they can be a highly effective way of drawing readers into a story – particularly when they culminate in punchlines presenting a surprise sting in the tail – in news-writing they should generally be used as an exception rather than a rule. In contrast, they are one of many conventions that have become highly prevalent in features, as the next chapter demonstrates.

News Language: Brevity, Clarity and Plain English

Of all forms of written journalism, news stories tend to be the shortest in length. To this extent, more is expected of them in fewer words – leaving them little room for redundant phrases, adjectives, or repetition. The importance of brevity and clarity in more general terms – and the use of active verbs and syntax in *all* types of article – is examined in detail in Chapter 8. However, it is worth touching on briefly at this stage, in relation to a particular aspect of journalistic writing which can prove hugely frustrating for news editors (and, by extension, readers) if it is not handled with care. Given the pressures faced by news reporters to explain sometimes complex stories in very few words, while writing them up – and, these days, uploading them – to ever-tighter and more numerous deadlines, it is very easy for them to slip into the habit of repeating received terms and phrases, without pausing to consider whether the same facts and/or opinions might be expressed in a simpler, more elegant way. While it is not the job of journalists to 'put words in people's mouths', and they should guard against oversimplifying genuine complexity by dumbing down the *detail* of a story, at times it is necessary for them to 'translate' jargon, 'officialese' and other technical terminology by finding suitable synonyms that will make it easier to understand without compromising on substance.

The onus placed on reporters to avoid blandly repeating the 'corporate-speak' routinely trotted out today by officials in both public and private sectors is often characterized as a pursuit of 'plain English' – a term owing its origins to George Orwell's influential 1946 essay 'Politics and the English Language', in which he railed against the encroachment of 'ugly and inaccurate' written prose. Though his tract led to the publication, two years later, of a new guide designed to steer council workers, bank managers and politicians away from jargon – *Plain Words: A Guide to the Use of English* by senior civil servant Sir Ernest Arthur Gowers – more than seventy years later, journalists are still confronted daily with technobabble, gobbledygook and (especially) acronyms and abbreviations which mean little or nothing to anyone other than a small coterie of those 'in-the-know'. For the news journalist – up against the clock and with only a few hundred words, at most, to tell a whole story – such jargon presents a particular obstacle, but one it is incumbent on him or her to overcome.

2. THE FEATURE

IF NEWS STORIES ARE the main building-blocks of newspapers (and many magazines), features are the splashes of colour that give them life and lustre. Though the term has conventionally been used to describe wordier, 'longer-form' articles – from single-page spreads to sprawling colour pieces in Sunday supplements – today's features come in all shapes and sizes and are frequently as driven by pictures as by prose. As this book is primarily about the craft of journalistic *writing*, most of the emphasis of this chapter will be on 'prose-led', rather than 'picture-led', features. However, no consideration of the form as it stands today would be complete without a brief mention of some of the main types of shorter feature, from the 'Q&A interview' to the 'tried-and-tested' consumer piece framed around the 'road-testing' of a range of competing products that has become a staple of numerous men's and women's lifestyle, fashion and gadget magazines.

The main types of longer feature fall into three or four, at times overlapping, categories: issue-based and/or investigative features involving interviews with multiple contacts; multi-sourced news features or 'backgrounders'; and interview-led features or profiles, often focusing on single individuals. Before exploring each of these separately, however, it is important to explode one popular myth about features. Although the most immediately 'newsworthy' feature articles tend, by definition, to be backgrounders, a common misapprehension about features in general is that, unlike news stories, they do not need to be rooted in 'the here and now'. This could not be further from the truth: for *any* type of feature (particularly a longer one) to engage readers and persuade them to invest time in reading and responding to it, there needs to be a highly topical subject at its core. Most print magazines (traditionally the main outlets for features) are periodical in nature, meaning that they only come out weekly, monthly or even quarterly – and this puts even more pressure on their editors to ensure that the content of any particular edition is timely and relevant. So, before pitching a feature idea to a commissioning editor, let alone plunging into the time-consuming business of researching and writing it, first ask yourself this: what is it about this subject that justifies a feature-length article at this particular point, rather than in six months' time – or, indeed, six months ago?

Issue-Based Features and News Backgrounders

Just as all features should be topical, so, too, should they contain enough *substance* to 'justify' their length. This is especially true of features, the primary purpose of which is to tackle matters that are the subject of popular debate and/or provide a more nuanced and considered exploration of the background to an issue currently in the news. Given that most news stories are written in fewer than 500 words – and some are considerably shorter, especially online, where journalists are often called on to save readers the hassle of having to scroll down the screen or click on successive pages – 1,000- or 2,000-word articles need to take full advantage of their relative size to pack in as much detail, colour and (where appropriate) description as possible. Having thousands of words to play with, then, is not an excuse to be twice as verbose as the news-writer who has to sum up the nub of the story your feature is based on in 300 words. Rather, it is incumbent on you to infuse your article with more *depth* and *insight* than can possibly be contained in a short report and (when exploring a complex or contentious issue), more data, quotes and opinions from a *wider range* of sources.

All that said, one of the most 'fun' aspects of feature-writing is that it gives journalists the chance to break free, even if only temporarily, from the structural straitjacket of news. With two or three times as many words at your disposal as a reporter (and occasionally even more), you will be forgiven for feeling a little liberated, and for indulging yourself with the odd linguistic flourish. Indeed, a common request from feature editors, in addition to their demand for more 'facts and figures' to explain and contextualize a subject, is that their writers should lace their articles with 'colour' and 'texture'. For this reason, features benefit more than any other type of article from the efforts of their writers to 'get out of the office' and visit the places and people they are preparing to write about in the flesh (a once-routine freedom today's news reporters are seldom permitted). The more first-hand knowledge you acquire of the locations, organizations and individuals about which you are planning to write, the more three-dimensional and believable will be the quality of your prose. When faced with the task of writing a lengthy piece of journalism, you should always be thinking about how you can 'entice' readers in and, having done so, persuade them to keep reading to the end. One way to do this is to imbue your writing with a sense of place – describing the sights, sounds and personalities you encountered so vividly that readers feel as if they can see, touch, smell or even taste them for themselves. At the risk of labouring a point, in today's frenetic world – one in which we are constantly besieged by competing distractions as we battle to gain the maximum benefit from our ever-more finite leisure time – it is more vital than ever for long-form writers to make their work polished, evocative and compelling.

Structuring Issue-based Features – Some General Conventions

Unlike with news stories, there is no widely accepted 'formula' for structuring features. In fact, within reason, there is no man-ifestly 'right' (or 'wrong') way to write one at all. This is not to say, however, that feature-writing is devoid of general ground-rules: depending on the category of feature they are working on, journalists will tend to fall back on one or other of a fairly limited range of devices when deciding how to frame their opening paragraphs, fill in the main body of the article and, perhaps most crucially, round it off. Indeed, before going any further it is worth pausing momentarily to emphasize this latter point: unlike news stories, which generally 'run out of steam' towards the end, as less important details are tucked in, the convention with features is that, like well-structured essays, they should have a clear beginning, middle and end. Almost as much effort (and imagination) tends to go into 'wrapping them up' neatly – tying up loose ends and/or giving readers a sense of closure at the end – as it does into grabbing them with an eye-catching, diverting or intriguing intro. This process of carefully crafting feature intros and outros, and getting from A to B by way of an interesting and informative middle, is popularly known as 'frame and fill'.

Small is Beautiful

One effective device commonly used by feature-writers to ensnare readers is to 'start small', before gradually opening out their articles onto the broader canvases they ultimately intend to cover. In the case of an issue-led feature, this might be achieved through the use of, say, a poignant quote from an individual or family affected by it – or the arresting image of a specific incident or encounter that *illustrates* the wider issue(s) the piece will go on to address. Take the following example from *Society Guardian*, which begins with a small-scale scene – that of a group of children huddled around a nursery teacher reading from an Apple iPad – before opening out into a discursive feature focusing on the merits and pitfalls of tablet computers being used in place of printed books in the classroom:

> Four small preschool children are sitting in a semi-circle around their teacher, in a large, bright room in a Georgian

house in Bath. The nursery belongs to the Snapdragons chain, one of the first in the UK to offer iPads to its children soon after the tablet was launched in April 2010. The shelves are full of books, but the children are not looking at books. They are listening to their teacher, Amy Porter, read aloud an interactive story from an iPad about Zub the monster.

(Paula Cocozza, 'Are iPads and tablets bad for young children?',
The Guardian, 8 January 2014)

In the remainder of her opening paragraph, writer Paula Cocozza goes on to show us the *level* of attention the children are investing in the electronic tool – describing how they 'bend towards the screen as if its glow were pulling them closer' and how the iPad 'disappears from view beneath four heads of supremely shiny hair'. Then, after a short bridging paragraph – which sketches in, for the previously uninitiated, a brief history of the rise in popularity (and sales) of tablets – she opens up her narrative to explicitly spell out the true *scale* of what her feature is about. The success of this 'start small, go large' approach owes much to the way the reporter hits readers with the following 'punchline' at the end of an extended dropped intro:

If you are an adult in possession of both a tablet and children, the children are likely to take possession of the tablet. According to Ofcom's latest report on the subject, household ownership of tablet computers has more than doubled from 20% in 2012 to 51%; where there are children in those households, they tend to be users too. When the Common Sense Report on media use by children aged up to eight in the US was published last autumn, it found that as many children (7%) have their own tablets as adults did two years ago (8%).

(Ibid.)

However, 'starting small' is only one way of approaching features focusing on popular issues. As both news backgrounders and more general issue-based features frequently centre on serious social or political topics, such as health, education and the economy, it is sometimes appropriate to adopt a more direct rhetorical device. Take this example from *The Economist:*

> BOOM times are back in Silicon Valley. Office parks along Highway 101 are once again adorned with the insignia of hopeful start-ups. Rents are soaring, as is the demand for fancy vacation homes in resort towns like Lake Tahoe, a sign of fortunes being amassed. The Bay Area was the birthplace of the semiconductor industry and the computer and internet companies that have grown up in its wake. Its wizards provided many of the marvels that make the world feel futuristic, from touch-screen phones to the instantaneous searching of great libraries to the power to pilot a drone thousands of miles away. The revival in its business activity since 2010 suggests progress is motoring on.
>
> ('Has the ideas machine broken down?', *The Economist,* January 2013)

Far from adopting a 'start small' approach, this issue-based feature opens with broad brush-strokes – painting bold scenes of economic rejuvenation across a sweeping canvas that, with its unabashed historical allusions, is as wide as it is long. Although it stops short of quoting precise statistics (as news features sometimes do), the article is drawing us in not with an image evoking closeness or intimacy but with a panoramic sense of *scale.* All the more impact, then, when the second paragraph turns the tables by adopting the following '*end*-small' approach to demonstrate that – whatever the big picture seen from afar might suggest – for many *individual* businesses located in Silicon Valley, any post-crash recovery still feels like a distant prospect:

> So it may come as a surprise that some in Silicon Valley think the place is stagnant, and that the rate of innovation has been slackening for decades. Peter Thiel, a founder of PayPal, an internet payment company, and the first outside investor in Facebook, a social network, says that innovation in America is 'somewhere between dire straits and dead'. Engineers in all sorts of areas share similar feelings of disappointment. And a small but growing group of economists reckon the

economic impact of the innovations of today may pale in comparison with those of the past.

(Ibid.)

In this case, then, the tactic being used to *keep* readers hooked is a cunning inversion of the more typical 'start small, go large' approach. When it can deliver a twist as effective as the one seen here, this 'start large, go small' conceit proves highly effective – and acts as yet another illustration of how much more varied, and less rule-bound, the practice of feature-writing is, compared to news.

Packing a Punch

Whichever intro style you opt for when writing a particular feature, however, there is one rule of thumb that applies to all issue-based pieces: at some point in your feature's first few paragraphs, you will have to deliver a punchline spelling out to readers *exactly* what the feature is 'about'. In the case of features, this all-important punchline – whether it comes two, three or even five paragraphs into an article – is known as the *nutshell paragraph*, or *nut-graph*. In both the previous examples, the nut-graph is the paragraph in which the writers, respectively, 'go large' and 'go small', and this tends to be the case for all such features. Whether they choose to switch from the particular to the general, or the general to the particular, issue-based features typically use their opening gambit to 'set the scene' for the main *angle* of the article – and spell out that angle in their nut-graph. Thus, the 'go-large' section of the *Society* feature (see pp.46–7) culminates with the paragraph in which the writer reels off a list of facts and figures emphasizing the level of children's interest in, and adoption of, tablet computers, while the 'go-small' chunk of the *Economist*'s contrasts the 'marketing-friendly' image of a go-getting, resurgent Silicon Valley with the grassroots reality of disaffected, low-morale IT companies.

The 'Circular' or 'Diamond' Feature: From Beginning to Middle, and How to End it

Once you have 'opened out' (or 'focused in') your feature, and perfected your nut-graph, your task is to get down in writing all the most relevant and newsworthy material you have gathered by interviewing sources, digging out statistics and conducting any other forms of primary and secondary research, in a logical and engaging sequence. Again, unlike news stories, the internal structure of features is not at all prescriptive: there is no 'inverted pyramid' to follow and there may be any number of (legitimate) 'paths' along which to lead readers, step by step, towards your denouement. A tip often repeated by leading practitioners is that feature-writers need to 'take command' of their material – spending as much (if not more) time looking back over their notes and quotes, and gathering their thoughts, as they do putting pen to paper. Taken together, the time spent researching the feature, transcribing any recordings or short-hand notes and determining the most suitable form in which to tell your story can be likened to a long-distance run – with the writing-up process equivalent to the final few laps of the park before you cross the finishing-line. An issue-based feature – which is of value only insofar as it succeeds in examining a subject affecting a number of people in sufficient *depth* – stands or falls on the quality and thoroughness of its research. In journalistic terms, this often means lengthy phone calls, email exchanges and/or face-to-face meetings with informed contacts, and efforts to obtain quotes and opinions from those representing a spectrum of different views on the matters concerned. Superficial web searches or rehashes of information included in earlier articles – derisively known as 'cuttings jobs' – will leave you with material too thin and superficial to provide a foundation for your piece. Not for nothing do journalists often remark that, once they have 'broken into' the writing stage and established a rhythm, there is an immense sense of relief that they have finally reached this point.

Assuming you *have* done your research properly, how should you structure your feature from the nut-graph down?

Depending on the subject of your feature, one way to navigate your way through this stage of the process is to think of it as a series of 'chunks' of discrete but related details and information, or even a succession of 'scenes' – much as screenwriters and film directors use 'story-boards' and scene breakdowns to map out their plots and camera scripts. A feature focusing on the question of sustainable immigration levels, for example, might move from a vivid opening depicting the persecution faced by someone who has recently entered the country and applied for immigrant status through a nut-graph stressing the overall scale of demands for passports and visas to the first of a series of quotes from different critics of the system (for example, from the perspective that the conditions imposed on prospective immigrants are unfairly harsh or unduly lenient). Having 'made the case' for one side or the other in this way – as a news reporter will 'front-load' a story with quotes and/or statistics arguing 'for' or 'against' something, in support of his/her intro angle – the writer will next need to introduce some *balance*, by first explaining that these views tell only 'one side of the story' and then 'showing' that this is the case, by bringing in a stream of facts, quotes and opinions that contest the dominant viewpoint suggested by the previous few paragraphs.

But this is just one approach. A different take is to adopt what (to revive an earlier metaphor) might be described as a 'journey' structure – leading the reader, as if by the hand, through a more or less linear, perhaps even chronological, unfolding of events or developments. Take the immigration example described previously: an alternative way of treating this same subject might be to, say, follow the progress of an aspiring immigrant as he or she goes through successive stages of the application process for British citizenship. Another would be to shadow the passage of such a person on the odyssey from their country of origin to their destination – tracing their trajectory as they board ships or planes, and battle through customs and immigration controls – in a more literal, step-by-step way.

These two contrasting, but equally legitimate, examples of how to approach a single feature demonstrate just how flexible and varied feature structures can be. For this reason, features

- more than any other type of article - should always be approached on an individual case-by-case basis, and it may not become clear to you how best to frame and fill a particular piece until the point at which you sit down to start writing. A useful (but by no means definitive) way to navigate your way through this process is to keep an eye (and ear) out, at all stages of the research and planning process, for a narrative or thematic strand that might help you weave the piece together in an elegant and engaging way. Once you have identified this thread, and are confident it is the right one (or as good as any other), you need to take a leap of faith and commit yourself to the route map it offers you - much as ancient Greek hero Theseus put his trust in a ball of string as he plunged into the Minotaur's labyrinth. This crucial stage in the process of 'breaking into' your feature is more about sensitively sifting the material you have gathered and, having done so, trusting in your 'journalistic instinct' to make the best use of it than it is finding some sort of perfect formula. Even feature-writers will normally be working to deadlines, so, while it is no bad thing to aspire to perfection, achieving it is seldom possible.

Where it *is* possible to be more prescriptive, though - especially in relation to issue-based features - is in describing the conventions popularly used to round them off. Unlike news stories, which front-load the most newsworthy and important information in their opening paragraphs and tend to be 'subbed from the bottom' when space is tight, features need to reward those who persevere to the end. For this reason, one common trick is for the writer to bring features 'full circle', in an effort to give them a sense of finality or closure: a formation sometimes likened to that of a diamond! They can do this either by following their central thread through to some sort of 'conclusion' - a salient observation or rhetorical flourish, perhaps, which somehow 'sums up' what the readers (and writer) have 'learnt' or 'discovered' during the course of their narrative journey - or, more literally, by returning to the image, scene or idea with which the piece initially opened.

The *Society* article quoted earlier on pp.46-7 offers one example of how to achieve this closure. Returning from her exploration of the wider issues arising from the popularity of tablet computers among children to a more intimate scene (albeit a different one to that she began with), Cocozza signs off with the last-minute twist that, for all its attractions, the iPad still presents one cause of frustration to its young fans: ultimately, it is no replacement for friends:

> Perhaps the tablet was secretly designed with children in mind as much as – or, who knows, more than – adults. Perhaps that would explain why children enjoy, unintimidated, all its potential – and instinctively understand its limits too.
> 'So you can basically do whatever you want to do on an iPad?' I ask Moin.
> 'Ye—es,' he says, hesitating.
> Then he adds, in a consoling voice, as if it's best I learn the bad news now: 'But you can't make it come alive. You can't make the iPad come alive.'

(Paula Cocozza, *The Guardian*, 8 January 2014)

A more straightforward example of a 'conclusion-style' approach is illustrated by *The Economist* piece, which rounds off with this measured assessment of the conflicting evidence it has encountered for the, by turns, stuttering and accelerating nature of Silicon Valley's recovery:

> In the end, the main risk to advanced economies may not be that the pace of innovation is too slow, but that institutions have become too rigid to accommodate truly revolutionary changes—which could be a lot more likely than flying cars.

(*The Economist*, 12 January 2013)

By contrast, the following two extracts from a feature in the *Independent on Sunday* by Cole Moreton demonstrate how poignant and striking a more overtly circular approach can be. In the opening paragraph of the article, which focuses on the tragic death of an 18-year-old soldier just two weeks after being posted to Basra in war-torn Afghanistan, his father reflects on his fun-loving persona, mistakenly using the present tense to refer to him, despite the fact he has died. In the second extract, taken from the feature's concluding paragraph, Moreton returns to the father – who, this time, ruminates bitterly on what he sees as his son's 'pointless' sacrifice. The intro reads:

'Jamie Hancock was a charmer, a good-looking boy with the physical confidence of someone who loved to box. Last time he was home in Lancashire he made the girls at Barbarella's nightclub giggle with his usual armoury of flirtatious one-liners, then showed them pictures of himself in uniform. "He's not a gob, but he can get on with anyone," said his father Eddie yesterday, before stopping himself. "I have to talk as if he is still alive. I have to think he is just on a tour of duty. I can't cope any other way.'

(Cole Moreton, 'Remembrance Sunday Special: Remember Jamie Hancock', *Independent on Sunday*, 12 November 2006)

The article concludes with the following passage:

Jamie Hancock was a bold, strong, passionate soldier of the sort who has given the British Army victory throughout history. He was a teenager from an army family and an army town. Jamie Hancock could have died at Dunkirk, the Somme or even Waterloo. But he didn't. 'He was in the wrong place at the wrong time,' said his father. 'I understand that sometimes people who serve have to die. That is not what gets me. It is that the reasons for his being there, for any of them being there and dying, seem so totally pointless.'

(Ibid.)

Doing the Introductions: Interview-based Features

Like backgrounders and other issue-based features, ones that focus largely or entirely on interviews with single individuals – whether celebrities, politicians or members of the public who have somehow found themselves the subject of journalistic attention – often tend to 'start small' and expand their horizons later. A typical opening quote or image, then, will say something bold about their opinions, their mood or their appearance on a particular day, while the main body of the piece will open out into something, by turns, more three-dimensional and situated. On the one hand, it will need to show (or remind) readers, in general terms, who its subject *is*; on the other, why he or she is deserving of interest or attention *at this particular time*. In this respect, then, interview-led features require just as much background and context as those revolving around wider themes or debates. Where they differ, though, is in the degree of onus they place on their writers' ability to transport their readers 'into the room' alongside them. For interview-led features to succeed, they need to conjure up impressions of their subjects so layered and/or vivid that readers are left feeling as if they have met them in person.

When written up, interview-led features conventionally appear in one of two formats. One is the 'write-through' feature: a piece of continuous prose, like the articles examined previously, which is used as much to *describe* the interviewee (in the words of the interviewer) as to relay what he or she actually *says*. The alternative approach is the 'Q&A': a more literal (and, as a result, less colourful) reflection of the outcome of the interview itself, which reproduces, more or less verbatim, the sequence of questions asked and the answers they provoked.

'Write-through' Interviews

It is often said that one of the main objects of features is to provide 'a good read'. In this respect, 'write-through' interview pieces win hands down over Q&As, as they offer the journalist a chance to show off his or her prose style and (to an extent) vocabulary free from the constraints of a simple question and answer format. There are, of course, hazards with this approach: when the shackles are off, there can be a tendency for journalists to 'let themselves go' that little bit too much, producing copy that is over-florid, verbose or even pompous as a result. While it feels understandably liberating to be allowed to inject more 'life' into one's writing – even to experiment, up to a point, with different forms and styles – it is all-too easy to slip into the bad habit of mistaking colour for purple prose.

Besides this danger – one faced by *any* journalist tasked with penning a lengthy article – write-through interviews also present a further hurdle. This is the need for the writer to include *observations* about the interviewee – their appearance, manner, mood etc. at the time of the interview – without appearing to pass *judgement* on them. Just as news reporters are expected to relate their stories in a neutral voice that avoids comment or opinion, feature writers must inject their prose with enough description for readers to be able to *picture* the interviewee, and get to understand something of how he or she 'ticks', while leaving it up to them to decide what they *think* of that person by the end.

A good example of how to strike the right balance between 'showing' readers what someone is like without 'telling' them what to think about him or her is this extract from a testy 2013 interview by *Guardian* writer Simon Hattenstone with the late singer-songwriter Lou Reed. Though Hattenstone opens the feature with a paragraph laying his cards on the table as a long-standing fan of Reed's music, during the course of the piece he takes us on a journey in which he is transformed from star-struck to speechless at the bullying bravado with which his interviewee parries and ridicules his questions. For most of the interview, Reed's intimidating persona is conveyed through a mix of verbatim quotes of his withering putdowns and grudging non-answers and Hattenstone's understated description of his aggressive mannerisms and body language, as the following passage illustrates:

He walks in silently, with swaggering B-movie menace. Of course, he'll act the hard man, but my copy of *NYC Man* is on the table and once we start talking about his greatest songs he'll relax. I know he will. Hey, I say, when I look at this record it makes me feel nostalgic for my youth, and I didn't even write the songs, so God knows what it does for you. He gives me a withering look. 'No, that's not what occurred to me.'

(Simon Hattenstone, 'Interviewing Lou Reed: not a perfect day', *The Guardian*, 19 May 2003)

But it is later in the feature that Reed is pictured at his most menacing. Hattenstone conveys this impression by using the first person to transport the reader directly into his shoes as he visibly quakes beneath a volley of verbal hectoring from his one-time idol:

... Reed makes me feel like an amoeba. I want to cry. Look, I was a huge fan of yours, I say. 'Was?' he sneers. I still am, I say, but I'm less sure by the second. I desperately try to stick to the music. Soon after his most commercial album, *Transformer*, Reed made his least-commercial record, *Metal Machine Music*, an album of feedback. Some critics said it was his joke on the pop business. Is there any validity in that? 'Zero.' Is it something he can enjoy? 'Well, I can.'

(Ibid.)

And, far from pulling back from the encounter, Hattenstone continues to crank up the tension still further – largely using Reed's give-nothing, wilfully hostile and obtuse dialogue to tell (or, rather, show) the story for him:

Which of his songs does he like best? 'I don't have a favourite.' Favourite album? 'I like all of them.' Warhol, the Velvet Underground's mentor, believed that art shouldn't be tinkered with to appease the market. Did he teach Reed to value his own work? 'It was great that Andy believed in us.' Warhol fell out with Reed before his death, complaining that he never gave him any video work. I ask Reed if he wishes they could have made up before he died. 'Oh, personal questions again.'

(Ibid.)

The article reaches its climax in, appropriately, the tetchiest and most petulant of rebuffs:

> But isn't the music shaped by his experiences and relationships? 'Don't the people you're around shape the music, is that what you're saying? Everything does.'
> So why won't you talk about them? 'You're not going to leave off that, are you? OK, let's not do it. We're not getting along. OK. You want to ask questions. I told you I can't do it so I can't do it. Thanks a lot. So I'll see you.' He's off.

> (Ibid.)

As we shall learn in Chapter 10, the first person can be an overused device and, more importantly, a distraction from the main point of a feature – with the lazy and unimaginative journalist effectively making *him or herself* the subject of a piece that purports to be about someone (or something) else. In this case, though, the conceit works a treat, as Hattenstone largely refrains from personalizing his encounter with Reed directly until the second half of the article – by which time he has already done more than enough to persuade us that he is in the presence of a tormented (and tormenting) genius. Like all the best interview-led features, what this example demonstrates is that the fluidity of the 'write-through' format allows writers the freedom to convey a much richer, more three-dimensional character portrait than is generally possible using a rigid Q&A framework. What was the interviewee wearing when you met them? Were they smart or scruffy? Did they look older, younger, or (in some other way) different from how they usually appear on stage, screen or in the papers? Did they seem happy, sad, friendly, hostile, enthusiastic – or bored? Had they just dashed in from a rehearsal – or the pouring rain? Were they suffering from jet-lag after a long-haul flight? Did they start out moaning about the weather, a hangover or last night's football results? While it is possible to convey *some* of this information in a Q&A, write-through features offer the flexibility to present it in a less stilted, more lively and visual way.

Q&As – When (and When Not) to Use Them

As Q&As allow little scope for journalists to demonstrate their writing skills, the secret to making them work is ensuring that they pose sufficiently searching and incisive questions. There is nothing more lame and insubstantial than the Q&A interview with a famous figure that falls back on pointless and/or random questions – for instance, raking over already well-trodden ground with which readers are likely to be familiar, or, worse still, exchanging inconsequential small-talk or asking them about their first kisses or favourite colours. Equally inadequate are the Q&As whose answers appear scripted (often because they *are* – and invariably by the celebrity's publicist rather than the interviewee him- or herself). When neither questions nor answers breathe any 'life' into the interview subject, or tell us anything about them we didn't know beforehand, there is little or nothing left for us to take away from an article, besides a sense of having wasted the last few minutes reading it.

When done well, however, a Q&A can be highly effective. Journalists who manage to gain access to elusive interview subjects, and aren't afraid to ask them difficult or probing questions, can provoke strong, surprising and, at times, highly revealing responses. On such occasions, whether or not interviewees actually *answer* questions may ultimately be immaterial, as the ferocity of their reactions – and/or their refusal to do so – can speak volumes about their character and personality, in so doing 'showing' readers a great deal about them. Indeed, if their responses are sufficiently punchy, barbed and/or amusing, the Q&A format can act to the article's *advantage* – by emphasizing the wit and eloquence of their ripostes, explanations and anecdotes, without requiring readers to wade through all the prose 'packaging' in which they might otherwise be buried. In such circumstances, Q&As also give journalists a chance to show off their interview technique, by reproducing the precise wording of the questions that *provoked* such interesting replies. Not for nothing did Hattenstone revert to a quasi-Q&A style for some of the later, most striking, exchanges in his torrid interview with Reed.

The following excerpt from a Q&A interview in *The Observer* newspaper is a good example of how an upfront, occasionally even audacious, questioning style can tease out answers which – even if they do not quite tell us everything we would nosily like to know about someone – offer *glimpses* of revealing detail about (in this case) quite personal topics. As the starkness of the Q&A format emphasizes, journalist Andrew Anthony does not baulk at asking his interviewee, then-BBC economics editor Stephanie Flanders, searching questions about various aspects of her private life – including her privileged public-school upbringing and time spent at the University of Oxford:

> '[Q] You went to St Paul's, the independent girls' school, in west London, and then Oxford. Do you think privilege has too much bearing on education and achievement?
> [A] I don't think you'll find anyone who's comfortable with the idea that the 6%, or whatever it is, who go to public school occupy such a large number of the places at Oxford and Cambridge and so many of the slots in public life. Social mobility certainly doesn't seem to be getting any better....'

> (Anthony, 'Stephanie Flanders: I'm the black sheep of my family',
> 20 February 2011)

There is one other kind of situation in which a Q&A approach works well. This is when the interviewee is so garrulous and opinionated that he or she needs little prompting to launch into a colourful tirade or anecdote, and when what he or she says is so interesting that it seems a shame to 'interrupt' their flow by weaving in chunks of third-person prose. With the Hattenstone–Reed interview, this approach would not have worked – largely because Reed said so little (or so little of any real clarity or meaning) that it was left to the description of his attitude and actions, and Hattenstone's reactions to them, rather than any words he actually *uttered*, to give the article its lustre. By contrast, the following extract from a Q&A with Pakistani-cricketer-turned-political-activist Imran Khan in *New Statesman* magazine shows how an erudite and articulate interviewee can so dominate an interview (in a positive way) that it is best to leave him or her to put things in his or her own words, with questions limited to periodic, if salient, prompts and the journalist otherwise taking a backseat:

> Mehdi Hasan: Should Pakistan receive international aid?
>
> Imran Khan: When Pakistan came into being, it was in a desperate situation, so it needed aid. But it should have been a temporary measure, like the Marshall Plan for Europe. Unfortunately, Pakistan became dependent on aid and that is where our problems started, because the ruling elite use aid to finance their lavish lifestyle rather than [address] a temporary problem of balancing your fiscal deficit, your expenditure and your revenues. We never had an austerity programme in Pakistan, so all this aid basically financed the elite and they got hooked on to it. There was no readjustment. The current government is the most corrupt in our history. If it wasn't for aid, this government would have collapsed.
>
> Hasan: What damage has it done?
>
> Khan: There are two problems with it. First, it stops us making the reforms to restructure our economy. If you have a fiscal deficit, you will be forced to cut your expenditure and you will do everything to raise your revenues. This important development did not take place, because of aid. Second, IMF loans. These two things have propped up crooked governments who have used the poor to service the debt through indirect taxation. The poor subsidise the rich in Pakistan. The ruling elite just don't pay taxes – all the taxes are paid by the common people.
>
> (Mehdi Hasan, 'The aid Q&A: Imran Khan', *New Statesman*, 20 June 2012)

In this case, Khan 'hijacks' what might otherwise have been a worthy but lifeless Q&A with an informed and passionate sermon about political and economic corruption in Pakistan. To have incorporated his remarks into a 'write-through' feature structure would have necessitated heavily editing them – for reasons of space alone – arguably undermining their impact in the process. In this instance, then, it is not the quality of the interviewer's *questioning* that gives the piece its value (Khan needs little nudging to lead him, logically, from one point to the next), but his willingness to sit back and let the author get things off his chest, only occasionally pressing him for more clarity. This 'less is more' strategy – directing an interview, but remembering the reader wants to hear what your *interviewee* has to say, not you – can be a highly effective addition to a journalist's toolkit, and here pays dividends.

By way of contrast, the following extract from an interview in the *Daily Star* newspaper with actor Aaron Paul, star of cult television drama *Breaking Bad*, demonstrates all the pitfalls of more insubstantial Q&As. Though it does not appear 'scripted' as such – the interviewee speaks fairly naturalistically and 'sounds' like the actor – the deferential, occasionally irrelevant, line of questioning creates the strong suspicion that it was vetted in advance by Paul's publicists to ensure maximum focus on his new movie (the interview's premise) and minimal opportunity for the journalist to pose any trickier or more wide-ranging questions:

[Q] Are you into cars?
[A] Yeah, who isn't into cars, right? I mean, I'm really into the more classic vintage muscle cars than these newer super cars, but yeah, I definitely love cars.
[Q] It must have been fun being able to drive some of the most iconic muscle cars.
[A] Yeah, I've been driving around in all kinds of cars and it's great. I want to take them all home with me. They won't let me.
[Q] How fast have you gone?
[A] On set, maybe 80 miles an hour. Just on a city street. But in real life, I've gone much faster than that.
[Q] What was your first car?
[A] My first car was a 1982 Toyota Corolla. Gold color. Manual transmission. Didn't really work well. The trunk would fill up with water whenever it rained. But I loved that thing like no other.
[Q] Did it go at least 80 miles mph?

[A] Well, it could maybe get 80 miles an hour, barely. But that thing was my pride and joy for many years.

[Q] Who drives for you when you're not allowed to?

[A] Well, let me just tell you the only reason I am even a little remotely great in this film is because of Tanner Foust who, I think, is one of the most brilliant stunt drivers there is in this business. He's going to make me look badass. So, good on you Tanner!

[Q] What excites you most about *Need for Speed*?

[A] The story alone is so great, but the action sequences that we have are incredible. It's pretty remarkable. It's just getting more and more exciting day to day. It's great.

(Andy Lea, 'Q&A: 'Aaron Paul talks *Need for Speed*, stunts and fast cars', *Daily Star*, 14 March 2014)

As with all many other interviews with A-list celebrities, this Q&A is inherently limited in journalistic merit because it tells – or, rather, *shows* – us nothing 'new' about its subject.

From 'How-to' to 'Tried-and-tested' – A Brief Word on Some Common Consumer Features

Recent decades have seen an increasing emphasis on 'lifestyle' journalism. As consumerism has become an ever-more potent driving force of modern life, the appetite for articles focusing on new products, services, holiday destinations and leisure pursuits has grown exponentially – to such an extent that many magazines and national newspaper supplements are now dominated by features focusing on the latest fads and fashions. These consumer-oriented pieces are broadly split into two categories: 'how-to' and 'tried-and-tested' pieces.

Often (but not always) written as an experiential first-person piece, the 'how-to' feature takes readers on a voyage of discovery that introduces them to something they could buy, sign up to and/or otherwise try out for themselves. By definition, subjects covered by such pieces can be extremely wide-ranging: everything from paragliding and snowboarding to cookery classes and the marvels of sushi and raw-food diets has been subject to the 'how-to' feature treatment (in some cases repeatedly) over the past few years. While 'how-to' pieces are usually presented as 'write-through' articles, however, 'tried-and-tested' features tend to be more picture-led and (in prose terms) bitty. Again, adopting a strong consumer focus, these articles tend to centre less on purchasable *experiences* than products – which (by definition) the journalist will try out and, by turns, criticize or recommend to readers. The article will usually seize on a particular kind of product that is popular at the time – be it mobile smartphones or wide-screen television sets – and compare and rate (often out of five or ten stars) several of the latest models to appear on the market. In this respect, these pieces tend to resemble glorified reviews – a type of article explored in more detail in Chapter 6. But, while they can be witty and sharply written, within the constraints of often very limited word counts, tried-and-tested articles offer little opportunity for journalists to display any flair for prose. For this reason, they are arguably deserving of only passing reference, rather than close attention, in a volume of this kind.

3. PROFILES AND OBITUARIES

THE TERM 'PROFILE' IS defined by the Oxford English Dictionary as 'a short character sketch or portrait', and in many ways this is an apt description of the variant of features to which it lends its name. Framed, as they are, as insights into the personalities, foibles and achievements of particular individuals who are in the news at given points in time, in terms of focus, profiles share an obvious similarity with interview-led pieces. The two species differ, though, in one important respect: while interview-led features revolve around conversations *with* individuals (or groups of individuals, such as pop bands), profiles are articles that tend to talk *about* – rather than to – them. Indeed, if there is one person the profile-writer does *not* normally need to worry about tracking down directly it is the subject of his or her feature. Rather, interviews conducted for profiles tend to be with those who know something about and/or have strong opinions on the subject/their work – whether they know (or have known) them personally, once worked with them, or have studied and analysed their work.

The fact that profile-writers do not need to go to the trouble of speaking to their (more often than not famous) subjects themselves, however, does not necessarily mean profiles are 'easier' pieces to research and write than interview-led features. On the contrary, the most incisive profiles are invariably those that act as 'mini-biographies' – and, to this end, include direct quotes from authoritative sources the writer has managed to buttonhole only after considerable effort. The weakest profile-writers by far are those who skirt around the issue of having to track down interviewees by simply digging out file quotes about their subject from the archives. Lazy profiles that contain little or no evidence of primary research on the journalist's behalf are known, variously, as 'cut-and-paste efforts', 'puff pieces' or 'cuttings jobs' – and editors (and most readers) can spot them a mile off. Good profile-writing (and researching), by contrast, is nowhere near as easy as this. Not only does it take time to identify, and contact, suitable commentators whose views on a subject are worth including, but if that subject is a globally famous politician or celebrity, many of those best placed to recount anecdotes or otherwise comment on them are likely to be very well known and/or in demand (for which read 'evasive') themselves. The *Intelligent Life* article used later in this chapter to illustrate the chronological format many profiles take on the page contains quotes apparently obtained by the writer, first hand, from at least half a dozen well-placed sources who know the subject and/or have something authoritative to say about him. While this may be a somewhat extreme example, it is this level of commitment to sourcing fresh, informed and illuminating anecdotes and opinions for which diligent profile-writers should be aiming.

The increasingly personality-centred nature of mainstream journalism today means that profiles have become an ever-more popular form of 'fall-back' feature for newspaper and magazine editors. Put simply, on any given day, or in any week, there will always be somebody (if not *several* somebodies) featuring so heavily in the news that they make for obvious profile subjects. In Britain, where one objective of weekend national papers tends to be to offer a 'digest' of the most noteworthy stories from the previous seven days, the profile has become a mainstay of many Saturday and Sunday titles. Some, such as *The Observer* and the *Independent on Sunday*, often feature not one but two profiles of people who have, in the previous week, been (or will, in the coming week, be) significant figures in the news – typically in their news review and arts/culture sections. While profiles share many common traits (in terms of form and structure) with other types of feature, their growing prevalence means they are arguably worthy of a short chapter to themselves.

Showing, not Telling: Framing your Character Sketch

As with other forms of written journalism, profiles can only achieve their goal with a bit of imagination and lateral thinking on the part of the writer. The aim of profile-writers is to conjure up three-dimensional portraits of their subjects without sliding into amateurish hero worship or cynical character assassination – or merely trotting out, by rote, facts and quotes with which readers are already likely to be familiar. For this reason, they often adopt a 'less is more' approach – melding considered observation and anecdote with well-chosen quotes and opinions from third parties that 'sum up' key aspects of their subjects' personalities and achievements. Although some repetition of well-known biographical detail is unavoidable in the case of famous celebrities, politicians or sports stars, it is the task of the profile-writer to qualify and question (if not challenge outright) hackneyed or predictable portrayals – surprising readers with the originality of his or her 'take' on a well-known figure and, occasionally, adopting an overtly revisionist position. Strong profiles query received wisdom, point out inconsistencies and contradictions in the way their subjects have previously been depicted, or have sought to portray themselves, and present alternative views that (in the best examples) have seldom, if ever, been voiced before.

One way to do this is to alight on a singular image, opinion or anecdote that can be argued to epitomize the essence of your profile subject. For example, if she is a celebrated performer known for her understated screen and stage persona and, equally, her tendency to shun publicity, one way to introduce her at the start of a profile might be to have her skulking in the shadows in the wings of a theatre, wracked with stage-fright moments before she appears before the public, or coyly refusing to answer her dressing-room door as hordes of fans await her autograph outside. Another approach might be to *confound* your audience's expectations. Would the star described above really be any less beguiling (or intriguing) if she were a famously *charismatic* on-screen/stage performer who turns out to be surprisingly shy and reticent when met in person?

Whichever option you choose, your object should be to ensure people who finish reading your profiles come away feeling that they have *learnt* something new about the subject – and either changed or reinforced their prior opinions about them based on the fresh insight and perspective you have offered. In other words, they need to know more about the subject than they did at the outset. Profiles are less about affirming pre-conceived ideas and pre-formed prejudices than giving readers the information they need to be able to look upon (often renowned or notorious) individuals in a new light.

Casting your Profile: The Opening Gambit

As with other forms of feature, there is no absolutely right (or wrong) way to open a profile, but the more striking the 'feel' for a person you can evoke in your opening paragraphs, the more likely readers are to be drawn in and (provided you maintain the early momentum) persevere to the end. One form of introduction that can be effective draws on the 'dropped intro' approach described in Chapter 1 – a device that 'teases' the reader by initially holding back confirmation of precisely whom the article is about. The following example from the *Daily Telegraph* uses a dropped intro approach to 'surprise' readers with the incongruity of a lesser-known achievement of its profile subject, in so doing setting up what will become a running thread of the profile: the idea that, having started out as a literary maverick, the author Ian McEwan has grown more conventional, and less cultish, with age:

> Looking for Booker Prize-winners in the list of Britain's hundred bestselling authors of the past decade is a bit like trying to find jokes in a Virginia Woolf novel; but there is one. Nestling between Andy McNab and Wilbur Smith, Ian

McEwan comes in at number 37, having sold more than four million books here in the past 10 years.

(Jake Kerridge, 'Ian McEwan: Profile', *Daily Telegraph*, 19 February 2010)

Getting to Know You: The Case for Chronologically Driven Profiles

Besides their overarching structures, profiles have something else in common with other types of feature: the need for a central narrative thread to guide readers through and hold them together. Though this is by no means prescriptive, in the most general terms there are perhaps two main kinds of 'thread': the *thematic* and the *chronological*. To take the latter first, a chronological approach is commonly used for profiles focusing on individuals who are either entirely new to the spotlight or – despite having been 'movers and shakers' in their fields for some time – have rarely, if ever, been profiled before. A hypothetical example might be that of, say, a local newspaper profile on a rising soccer star who has just been offered trials by a Premier League football club. Though he is likely to have had a 'name' for his sporting prowess for some time among family, friends and classmates, to most readers he will be unfamiliar. In this case, once the profile's intro has done its job in sketching in who its subject is, the rest of the article is likely to benefit from a chronological approach, which takes readers, stage by stage, through his life and achievements to date. A profile of a once-famous but now long-forgotten (or seldom seen) film star or musician might equally benefit from this treatment, with the writer framing the profile as a sort of potted biography designed to 'jog the memories' of older readers and perhaps even evoke a sense of nostalgia for 'the good old days'.

The following extract from a profile of veteran Hollywood actress Dame Angela Lansbury, published on specialist movie website http://www.tcm.com, offers a good example of how a more overtly biographical approach, combined with a brief summation of the subject's career highlights, can be used to good effect to 'reintroduce' someone who was once more famous than they have been of late. Framed around the 'peg' of upcoming film showings on the Turner Classic Movies (TCM) film channel, the article goes to some lengths to (re)familiarize its audience with Lansbury's background and oeuvre:

> MGM put her in a strange assortment of roles. 'When I was a kid in Hollywood the producers didn't know what to do with me. That was the period of the ladies. I was very young and looked, shall we say, mature? I was chubby because I ate all the time: Fig Newtons, chocolate bars, fudge ... Someone decided I should be the youngest character actress in the business. I never had the chocolate-box looks they wanted for romantic leads in those days. So when I was in my twenties, I was in make-up to play beastly women in their forties and fifties'. Happily, she was given the rare chance to play a girl roughly her own age when she finally got the role of Sibyl Vane in *The Picture of Dorian Gray* (1945, which earned her another Best Supporting Actress nomination). And it was through her *Dorian Gray* co-star, Hurd Hatfield, that Lansbury met her second husband, Peter Shaw, who she married in 1949. They had two children and remained married until his death in 2003.
>
> (Lorraine LoBianco, 'Angela Lansbury: star of the month',
> www.tcm.com, January 2014)

A chronological thread can also take other forms, besides being framed around a biographical run-down of a profile subject's background or upbringing. Take this example, from *Intelligent Life*, in which Larry Gagosian, the influential art dealer, is profiled specifically in the context of his apparent elusiveness and unwillingness to converse with the media in person. Although the 2008 profile is framed around a thematic thread – in this case, the notion that, defying a global recession that has seen the bottom fall out of a previously buoyant art market, Gagosian's success story continues – it is structured, in large part, chronologically. For general readers less familiar with the enigmatic Gagosian, it contains a detailed résumé of his life and times, focusing on the steady expansion of his art empire from its humble beginnings to the seven, internationally famous, galleries he boasts today. And it is this chronology that forms the central narrative around which the rest of the article pivots, as the following opening paragraph illustrates:

> Gagosianopolis began modestly in 1975 on a patio in the Westwood Village neighbourhood of Los Angeles. Gagosian, then 30, was an English graduate from UCLA who had left one job as an assistant at the William Morris talent agency and another parking cars. He has said that his upbringing brought him no real contact with art. His father was an accountant and later a stockbroker, his mother a bit-part actress. As he explained in an early interview, he borrowed the $75 rent for the patio from her and sold framed posters for $15 each. He moved on to more expensive posters and mounted his first art exhibition the following year, in a former Hungarian restaurant rented for about $400 a month.
>
> By the early 1980s, Gagosian had a proper gallery space and became the LA outpost for artists like Eric Fischl, Richard Serra and Frank Stella, who were represented by New York galleries. But he was making most of his money by brokering deals between LA collectors, arranging for paintings to be plucked from the walls of one owner and rehung on the walls of another, while he pocketed the commission.
>
> (Sarah Douglas, 'Larry Gagosian: the art of the deal', *Intelligent Life*, spring 2008)

This strand is picked up again later in the feature, when it is reintroduced in the context of Gagosian's superhuman ability to conjure up profit and prestige, even in straitened times: the premise of the future. In this way, the profile fuses a *thematic* idea – about Gagosian's business acumen and resilience – with an underpinning narrative structure that draws heavily on the *chronological* approach adopted by profiles that introduce readers to someone (or something) new or little understood.

Thematic Profiles

A more conventionally *thematic* approach to profile-writing tends to be used when the subject of the piece is someone whose overall level of fame (or infamy) is such that he or she should already be well known to most readers. It would be pointless, for instance, for a national newspaper profile of a serving prime minister or president to waste too much space telling, or reminding, readers who he or she is – or, indeed, repeating oft-cited facts about his or her family, educational and/or professional background. Rather, as in the Ian McEwan profile quoted previously, the best linking thread is likely to be one that relates explicitly to the 'nature' of the publication, or section, in which it appears – and, by implication, the audience for which it is intended. To this end, it is likely to adopt an approach that knits together salient (if, at times, disparate) facts and observations about the subject in a more lateral way, drawing out general patterns and connections from the particulars of their lives and times. The following extract from a profile in the *Daily Mail* of acclaimed singer-songwriter Kate Bush offers another example of how the structure of a piece aimed at a specific market – in this case, readers of a mid-market tabloid with a middle-aged female target audience – can cohere around a thematic thread. This is the (well-rehearsed) 'mystery' surrounding the star's obsessive privacy:

> She said that just walking onto the stage made her 'incredibly nervous', and sure enough those standing close to her could see she was trembling under the spotlights. Her hands, encased in fingerless gloves, shook as they grasped her award.
>
> Her famously soft and high-pitched voice was hesitant and much lower when she gave her acceptance speech. But perhaps we should not be surprised, since it was musician Kate Bush's first public appearance in seven years.

> (Alison Boshoff, 'Obsessive secrecy, a £30m fortune and the trauma that drove Kate Bush into hiding', *Daily Mail*, 3 May 2012)

Thematic threads are also a particular mainstay of more specialist publications, whose readers will often be 'fannishly' familiar with key players in a field a more general readership might never have heard of. Though admittedly no stranger to the mainstream media, Arsene Wenger, manager of Premiership football club Arsenal, was profiled with little or no introduction (let alone biographical background) in specialist soccer magazine *FourFourTwo* in 2013. Instead, the writer chose to frame the whole piece around Wenger's 'superhuman' staying power in a managerial position he had held, through highs and lows, for eighteen years – while numerous lesser mortals have fallen by the wayside:

> We live in an age where coaches are professionally obliged to be superhuman. An age in which – with every tactical ploy questioned by the Twitterati, every team line-up challenged by bloggers and every performance scrutinised by a horde of headline-seeking pundits – a manager can feel as if they are at the epicentre of, to quote Martin Amis, a 'moronic inferno'.
>
> Football management has never been a job for the weak-kneed, indecisive or plain idle, but the ritual sacking of coaches this season suggests the pressure is greater than ever.
>
> (Paul Simpson, 'Analysing the superhuman resilience of Arsene Wenger', *FourFourTwo*, 10 December 2013)

Knowing Me, Knowing You: The First-person Perspective

An increasingly common approach to profile-writing is for the journalist to cast the piece in the first person – regaling readers with observations based on his or her first-hand knowledge of its subject. In such cases, writers may have sufficient material available from their own (direct and/or vicarious) experiences that they are able to dispense with the usual necessity to source anecdotes and opinions from third parties. Though many British-based newspapers and magazines still tend to prefer

features to be written in the third person, the practice of inserting oneself into articles is much more commonplace in America.
And, in the case of profiles, it has been used very effectively
in Britain, too – especially when it has helped illuminate an
elusive, mysterious or contentious figure about whom the writer
genuinely has privileged knowledge, based on his or her own
direct dealings or encounters. When a journalist of sufficient
stature and experience is given the editorial 'licence' to frame
a profile in this way, drawing on his or her personal anecdotes about the subject, the results can be highly memorable,
as illustrated by the following extract from a colourful, highly
personalized, profile styled as an 'epitaph' to former UK Prime
Minister Margaret Thatcher written by her biographer, the late
Guardian journalist Hugo Young, less than a fortnight before his
death:

> The first time I met Margaret Thatcher, I swear she was
> wearing gloves. The place was her office at the Department
> of Education, then in Curzon Street. Maybe my memory is
> fanciful. Perhaps she had just come inside.
>
> But without any question, sitting behind her desk, she
> was wearing a hat. The time was 1973. This was the feminine
> creature who, two years later, was leader of the Conservative
> party.
>
> (Hugo Young, 'Margaret Thatcher left a dark legacy that has still
> not disappeared', *The Guardian*, 8 April 2003)

With the air of a man intent on settling scores while he still has
time, Young goes on to launch into a strident, but carefully cal-
ibrated, attack on Baroness Thatcher's political motivations and
actions. Describing 'her greatest virtue' as 'how little she cared
if people liked her', he praises her single-minded pursuit of
bold policies including industry privatization and trade union
reform, while unreservedly condemning their long-term consequences – accusing her of an 'indifference to sentiment and good
sense' that 'brought unnecessary calamity to the lives of several
million people'. The reason Young gets away with such stark
criticisms – ones that in lesser hands might have come across as

unsubstantiated value judgements – is because, like all the best writers, he uses *evidence* to back up his conclusions. Amid the myriad historical details he cites to demonstrate the contradictions in Thatcher's legacy – for example, the fact she 'led Britain further into Europe, while talking us further out' – he repeatedly weaves in personal anecdotes to further support this assertion. In this way, he gives informed readers, already aware of the conflicted nature of some of Thatcher's policies, the benefit of a new insight into the contradictions in her as a *person* – for example, the curious fact that she 'continued for some reason to consider me worth talking to', despite his habit of writing 'columns of pretty unremitting hostility to most of what she did'. And, like many of the best features, the profile closes with a sense of 'circularity', ending with an image of Thatcher sitting down to write her memoirs thirty years after their first encounter that, among other things associated with her – from 'promises' and 'action' to 'hat' and 'handbag' – refers to the gloves she wore on that occasion.

Profiling 'Things', not People

As stated earlier, profiles do not always confine themselves to examining a single person. In the case of music magazines or newspaper sports sections, for example, it is not unusual to find profiles focusing on, say, whole pop bands or even football teams. In more specialist publications, this rule of thumb is sometimes extended further still, to entire companies or even bigger institutions. Take, for example, the following extract from a profile in *The Lawyer* – a business-to-business magazine aimed at people working in the British legal profession – which centres on a specialist firm of solicitors based in Brentwood, Essex:

> One of Wortley Byers' straplines sums up its philosophy: 'Life isn't always black and white. For the grey areas, you need clarity, fairness and understanding.' The firm aims to provide a service that unravels the complexities of law, shedding light on the grey areas so that if they do not quite end

up being black and white, they are at least comprehensible.

(Alex Wade, 'Firm profile: Wortley Byers', *The Lawyer*,
9 February 2004)

The aim of this kind of piece is far less to provide any form of 'entertainment' for its (highly specialist) readers than to *inform* them (albeit as engagingly as possible) about other 'movers and shakers' in their industry or sector. Whereas *FourFourTwo* is a 'special interest' *consumer* magazine – one eagerly bought, if not subscribed to, by football fans – the nature of *The Lawyer's* niche appeal is less one that meets the demands of enthusiasts for news and gossip than the *necessity* for those seeking to 'get on' in a given profession to stay informed about the activities of their competitors.

Profiling the Dead: Writing Obituaries

No chapter on profiles would be complete without reserving a brief word for obituaries. Though many profiles are predicated on a significant chapter in their subject's *life* – gaining or quitting a job, receiving an honour or award, or doing (or having done to them) something otherwise significant – perhaps the most obvious peg for a feature dedicated to a notable individual is the occasion of their *death*. Traditionally, the demise of a famous person will tend to be accompanied by either or both of two kinds of article: a 'death story', detailing the facts and circumstances surrounding the subject's passing in the style of a straightforward news piece, and a full-blown obit, which melds the structure and facets of a profile with the tone and emphasis of a tribute. While tabloid papers conventionally combine the news story and the tribute in a single piece, most broadsheets will have discrete obit sections. In addition to carrying a report in their news pages about the death itself, often in the same issue a space will be reserved for a fuller reflection on the person's life and achievements.

Although obits are structured and composed very similarly to profiles, there are some important differences in the ways they are approached. A mundane, if important, distinction is that, while the pay-off lines of profiles can be as varied as those of other types of feature, obits usually end more formulaically – with a sombre coda informing (or reminding) readers of the immediate family the dead person has left behind. This is normally couched, quite literally, as 'he/she leaves a husband/ wife/partner [insert name]' and, for example, 'three teenaged children', perhaps also followed by the latter's names and ages. Another convention is that obits are frequently written not by journalists per se but by friends or colleagues of – or authorities on – the deceased: in other words, precisely the sorts of people journalists would normally approach in order to obtain quotes about the subject for a profile. Though they are rightly used only in certain circumstances, where an editor manages to persuade a high-profile politician, celebrity or academic to write an exclusive obit for his/her pages, invariably at short notice, these can make for some of the best-informed and most emotional tributes. The following is highly personal 'sign-off' to an obit of Venezuelan president Hugo Chavez written by his fellow socialist, the Respect MP George Galloway, for Britain's *Independent*:

I knew him as a warm gregarious bear of a man, a force of nature.

My wife and I spent almost two weeks working in his presidential campaign late last year. It is heartbreaking to be writing what amounts to his obituary so soon after yet another of his great political triumphs. He will be remembered as a man who lived and died for his people, as a paratrooper, a tank commander, a president. Hasta siempre Comandante. Presente.

(George Galloway, 'Hugo Chavez's death is a body blow for the poor and oppressed throughout Latin America', www.independent.co.uk, 5 March 2013)

By far the most significant disparity between obits and more standard profiles, however, is the curious 'advantage' the former have in their ability to offer honest, warts-and-all portraits of their subjects. In many ways, obits represent the first opportunity for their writers to reflect on a much-loved (or derided) figure without fear or favour, exploring aspects of their personalities and/or (alleged) behaviour that may have remained largely unwritten while they were alive – if nothing else, because of the fear of litigation. Even in Britain, a country with notoriously strict libel laws, there is a long-standing acceptance that 'the dead cannot sue' for defamation, and while this should never be taken as a licence to spread scurrilous or unsubstantiated rumours simply because they might make 'a good story', in death the famous do bequeath journalists a certain amount of freedom to be candid and critical. The death, in April 2013, of Baroness Thatcher, for example, sparked as many instant condemnations of her political legacy as it did even remotely fulsome tributes, with the range of responses from journalists, former associates and adversaries proving so varied that they formed the basis of a whole book, Louisa Hadley's *Responding to Margaret Thatcher's Death* (2014). Amid a plethora of more reverent tributes published to mark the 2011 death of then popular television personality Sir Jimmy Savile, the *Daily Telegraph*'s was remarkable for its decision to revisit, albeit fleetingly, long-running rumours about his predilection for sexual relationships with children. The piece – written a full year before a television exposé would revive the allegations and prompt a slew of inquiries into years of alleged paedophile abuse by Savile at public premises ranging from NHS hospitals to Broadmoor Prison to the BBC – contained this understated but, with hindsight, significant passage:

> Savile always claimed that the key to his success on *Jim'll Fix It* was that he actually disliked children, although in later years he maintained that he had offered this explanation to allay any untoward suspicions that he liked them too much. Rumours of under-age sex circulated for some years, although the fact that no allegations of impropriety ever appeared in print seemed to confirm Savile's own insistence that he had 'no past, no nothing'.

> ('Obituary: Sir Jimmy Savile', *Daily Telegraph*, 29 October 2011)

Avoiding Hagiography

Mention of the dangers of allowing profiles to become too syc-ophantic and rose-tinted – the dominant judgement of Savile immediately after his death (all-too ironic, given what subse-quently came to light about him) was that of a loveable eccentric and 'tireless charity fundraiser' – brings us to the folly of hagi-ography. The role of a profile or obituary is not to lavish effusive praise (let alone deify) its subject – however virtuous and/or high-achieving he or she might have been. Rather, it is meant to present a balanced, reasoned and revealing portrait of *the whole person*, particularly that part of him or her that remained, for the most part, hidden from public view. Many of the individu-als referred to in this chapter are (or were) hugely high-profile figures, and far from publicity-shy or enigmatic. What value is there, then, in simply reeling off lists of their widely known talents and achievements – at best, telling us what we already know; at worst, airbrushing their histories and leaving us feeling somewhat queasy at the sentimentalism of what is meant to be a nuanced and objective article? Profile-writers and obitu-arists have a responsibility to delve beneath the surface of their subjects, opening up their more private sides to wider scrutiny and, at times, setting the record straight about them. This is why hagiography – defined by the Oxford English Dictionary as 'the writings of the lives of the saints' – has no place in their work, and it is properly authenticated *biographical* background detail to which they must ensure they adhere.

Beware the 'Hatchet Job'

For every hagiographer – shamelessly rewriting history to offer an airbrushed vision of the life and times of a flawed and divi-sive figure – there is a profile-writer consumed with disdain, resentment or jealousy towards his or her subject. Whereas hagiography might represent a breach of journalistic integ-rity, character assassination is more than just a question of ethical standards (important though these are). From a purely self-interested point of view, it has the potential to land the writer – and his or her publication – in serious trouble, as an unsubstantiated written attack on someone's character or personality can, in legal terms, be construed as malicious falsehood. Unlike the subjects of obituaries, living individuals can sue for libel if they feel a journalist's barbs have crossed the line into malice and/or tarnished their reputations in the eyes of 'right-thinking members of society generally' (to quote the somewhat arcane wording of defamation law). And, as the subjects of profiles are often famous (and therefore wealthy), and have much to lose if they allow serious criticisms or allegations to go unchallenged, they have a tendency to be highly litigious. Though rare, there have been a number of occasions when even experienced journalists have fallen foul of the laws on malice. In July 2011, for example, veteran columnist Lynn Barber lost a case against author Sarah Thornton in respect of a *Daily Telegraph* article about her book, *Seven Days in the Art World*.

Articles that lay into their subject in a vindictive way – rather than criticizing them with a more measured and balanced tone, and with some attempt to address their virtues as well as vices – are known in the industry as 'hatchet jobs'. And, while they are most often to be found in the guise of profiles (hardly surprising, given that such pieces are focused on people), they also crop up, at times, under the auspices of news backgrounders and, particularly, reviews. It is when a review veers away from the subject it is meant to be considering – i.e. a piece of work, such as a book, play, film or record – to directly criticize the artist behind it, and to do so in a *personalized* way, that it strays into the realms of the hatchet job. The following extract is a case in point. It is taken from a caustic 'review' of *By Nightfall*, a novel by Michael Cunningham, author of the Pulitzer Prize-winning *The Hours*, by *Observer* journalist Adam Mars-Jones. The write-up, which won *The Omnivore* website's 'Hatchet Job of the Year' prize in 2012 – actually a coveted award, intended to 'raise the profile of professional critics and to promote integrity and wit in literary journalism' – starts out with the following biting summation of what Mars-Jones regards as the folly of the book itself, which leads him to conclude that the author lacks confidence in the strength of his own characters and narrative:

> Nothing makes a novel seem more vulnerable, more naked, than an armour-plating of literary references. If you're constantly referring to landmarks, it doesn't make you look as if you're striding confidently forward – it makes you look lost. In a 20-page section of Michael Cunningham's new novel, *By Nightfall*, in which the hero Peter Harris, an art dealer, visits a faithful client, there are explicit references to: *The Magic Mountain*, John Cheever, *Death in Venice*, Donald Barthelme, Raymond Carver, Hawthorne and *Death of a Salesman*.
>
> (Adam Mars-Jones, '*By Nightfall* by Michael Cunningham – Review', *The Observer*, 23 January 2011)

While some (including *The Omnivore*) might consider such writing 'witty', as a rule it takes a particular panache to pull off a hatchet job, and they rarely work as pieces of disciplined journalism. More often, they come over as little more than 'cheap shots' at someone who happens to be a pet hate of their authors. As a result, they are best avoided.

4. REPORTAGE

FOR MANY JOURNALISTS, REPORTAGE is where the business of news-gathering and, especially, writing starts to feel more satisfying. Being commissioned or sent out of the office to write a 'colour piece' on a breaking news event or from a location at the centre of an unfolding or ongoing crisis offers a chance to loosen the chains of the news-desk, spring free from the straitjacket of 'hard' news reporting and spend time exploring, absorbing and crafting a more personal and impressionistic account of what you see, hear, touch and smell while doing so. Reportage is less about chronicling the 'nuts and bolts' of what is being said and done in a news situation (though the best of it achieves this, too) than giving readers a 'feel' for the news event, its key players or protagonists and their collective significance. In this respect, it bears a closer resemblance to feature-writing than straight reporting – often using licences that go with that territory, such as dropped intros, descriptive language and the present tense, to create a more tangible and immediate 'sense' of what is going on than is possible in the stilted, no-nonsense delivery characteristic of most simple news stories.

Take the following example of one of many daily dispatches by award-winning US-based *Guardian* reporter Suzanne Goldenberg from the frontline of what, in early 2003, was about to become the Iraq War. In the space of a handful of lines, Goldenberg deftly draws the reader into a tense Baghdad, where she is witness to a state of pregnant expectation about the imminence of the allied invasion:

> Reality finally came to Baghdad yesterday. Overnight, sandbags sprouted on football fields and roundabouts. In the evening the authorities rustled up yet another peace demonstration.
>
> The number of fatal car accidents seemed to surge, with drivers in a panic to get home, or to get out. Chemists sold out of valium. Queues at petrol stations broadened and lengthened in a country where fuel is ridiculously cheap and plentiful. The price of mineral water doubled. Tinned foods and packaged soups disappeared from supermarket shelves. Young couples rushed to get engaged. Workers stored the files and fixtures from Iraqi government office buildings.
>
> (Suzanne Goldenberg, 'Suddenly the Iraq war is very real', *The Guardian*, 19 March 2003)

A more straightforward news report would have concentrated on merely itemizing the hard 'facts and figures' of what was happening – or, in this case, *not yet* happening – as Iraqi citizens hunkered down for the siege ahead. Given that Goldenberg's account was framed around the expectation of an *impending* event, rather than the event itself, there would be little for general news reporters to get a 'handle' on at this stage. But does the absence of an immediate surge of troops and tanks over the horizon make Goldenberg's portrait any more powerful, or indeed 'newsworthy'? Rather, her skill (and the article's resultant readability) lies in its use of the small-scale and particular to conjure up an atmosphere of high tension and to symbolize and set the scene for the large-scale and general. In one especially striking paragraph she describes the actions of a young boy in a way that foreshadows, ominously, the conflict and carnage that lies ahead:

> In the kitchen of the Abdel Hamid family you could see it had arrived. A young boy, Amir, was making his own final preparations for the onslaught. He was performing the last rites of a four-year-old. In his hand he brandished a plastic

gun. Whacking the ammunition clip into the toy, he held it to his stomach and put on a fierce expression. Then he raised it to the heads of the surrounding adults. 'Where are my bullets?' he screamed.

(Ibid.)

This almost literary metaphor would have no place in a straight news story. Yet it demonstrates the peculiar potency of the best reportage, by distilling deeper lessons about human frailty and, in this case, the *inhumanity* of warfare from the microcosm of a scene of hurried preparation for Armageddon played out against an otherwise mundane backdrop of family domesticity.

Goldenberg and her ilk have many notable antecedents – from the earliest war correspondent, William Charles Russell of *The Times*, to fearless freelancer Seymour Hersh, whose most revered work is discussed later in this chapter. Few exemplars of war reportage, however, could turn a phrase with quite the lightness of touch and eye for detail of Richard Harding Davis, whose work for William Randolph Hearst (the newspaper tycoon who famously inspired Orson Welles' *Citizen Kane*) is among the most quoted by any Victorian or Edwardian journalist. Perhaps his most celebrated single article was the piece that came to be known as 'The Death of Rodriguez' – a master-class in colour writing which displayed the symbolism of a morality tale without once resorting to anything as clumsy as overt comment. The 'story', published in 1897 by Hearst's *New York Journal*, revolved around the last moments of a Cuban rebel executed for his part in a revolt against Spanish colonialists. As he approaches the spot where he is to be killed by firing squad, we observe the following:

It was very quickly finished ... The crowd fell back when it came to the square, and the condemned man, the priests and the firing squad of six young volunteers passed in, and the line closed behind them. The officer who had held the cord that bound the Cuban's arms behind him and passed across his breast, let it fall on the grass and drew his sword, and Rodriguez dropped the cigarette from his lips and bent and kissed the cross which the priest held up before him.

Even in his day, Harding Davis was something of a one-off. That this forensic slice of descriptive prose was included not in a book but in a 'routine' newspaper report makes it all the more remarkable – and all the more worthy of being highlighted in a chapter concerned with the power of reportage.

Reportage and 'Literary' Journalism

Given the 'writerly' nature of reportage, it is perhaps unsurprising that this kind of journalism has produced some notable authors, including novelists – or that, conversely, a number of famous fiction-writers have turned their hands to it. Ernest Hemingway, George Orwell and Graham Greene are among the celebrated literary stylists who worked for long periods as journalists, while the most well-known books by the likes of Truman Capote, Jack Kerouac and Hunter S. Thompson (often bracketed as novelists) were not works of fiction but, rather, extended, book-length reportage – or, in the latter two cases, 'Gonzo' journalism. More recently, journalist-novelists like Tom Wolfe have produced extensive bodies of non-fiction writing, often using the first person and abandoning any pretence at normative journalistic objectivity, under the banner of 'New Journalism'. Much of this, too, bears strong formal and stylistic similarities to reportage.

From Riis to Capote: Investigative Reportage, Eyewitness Narratives and the 'Story-tellers'

Among the very best ambassadors for reportage as a form of extended journalistic story-telling was George Orwell, whose ability to blend economical dialogue and description with short bursts of undiluted colour also fed into his comparatively small (but rightly celebrated) fictional output. In a classic scene-setter, from the opening chapter of *Down and Out in Paris and London* (1933), his novel-length memoir about his personal experience of poverty and unemployment, he memorably described a 'representative Paris slum', with its 'ravine of tall, leprous houses, lurching towards one another in queer attitudes, as though they had all been frozen in the act of collapse' and 'tiny BISTROs, where you could be drunk for the equivalent of a shilling'.

Leaving aside Orwell's skill in evoking the dinginess and squalor of his location – his use of the literary technique known as pathetic fallacy all but personifies the 'tall, leprous houses, lurching towards one another in queer attitudes' – he achieved a perfect mix of 'show and tell' in such passages. This one opened with the most vivid of images, *showing* us what the slum looks and sounds like, before using a more authoritative voice to *tell* us about the diverse inhabitants to which it is home ('facts' that, at this stage, we are expected to take on trust). But, for all its refinement in the hands of one of the most skilled journalistic stylists the twentieth century produced, Orwell's technique here was not entirely new. Some forty-three years earlier, the pioneering Dutch investigative journalist, Jacob Riis, had employed similar tactics – in his case, combined with one of the most vivid early exercises in what was to become known as 'photojournalism' – to persuade readers to share his own thinly veiled indignation over the condition of overcrowded New York tenements in his 1890 work, *How the Other Half Live*. In the following extract, note how he uses a similar 'show and tell' approach to describe how the 'tulips or early cabbages' of the 'stolid Dutch burgher' and the 'garden gate' swinging on its 'rusty hinges' were supplanted by 'a rear house', and then another, to ease the 'pressure of the crowds'. The precision of Riis' writing brings to life this years- or decades-long process as if we were watching it unfold in a film montage sequence:

> Still the pressure of the crowds did not abate, and in the old garden where the stolid Dutch burgher grew his tulips or early cabbages a rear house was built, generally of wood, two stories [*sic*] high at first. Presently it was carried up another story [*sic*], and another. Where two families had lived ten moved in. The front house followed suit, if the brick walls

were strong enough ... It was rent the owner was after; nothing was said in the contract about either the safety or the comfort of the tenants. The garden gate no longer swung on its rusty hinges. The shell-paved walk had become an alley; what the rear house had left of the garden, a 'court' ...

Though a more in-depth exploration of form and style is reserved for the second part of this book, it is worth stressing here that the freedom literary reportage allows journalists to be more colourful and less rule-bound in their writing does not give them an excuse to produce prose that is florid or overwritten. In fact, as the examples of Orwell and Riis show, much of the most effective literary reportage employs descriptive language that is sparing and understated. An even starker illustration is the scene-setter to Chapter 2 of Ernest Hemingway's *In Our Time* (1925), a collection of his journalism – some of it based on cables charting his eyewitness accounts from war-zones (in this case, north-western Turkey during the 1919–22 Greco-Turkish War). In it, the writer describes, with ice-cool detachment, observing the fleeing carts full of 'women and kids ... crouched with mattresses, mirrors, sewing machines, bundles', against a once regal backdrop of 'minarets stuck up in the rain out of Adrianople'. This sparse, pared-back prose acts as a perfect introduction to the 'anti-adjectival' style that typified many of his novels – and, among other things, led the literary critic Cyril Connolly to remark, somewhat unkindly, that he seemed 'unable to distinguish' between journalism and literature (the latter being, to Connolly, an altogether higher form of writing):

Hemingway's short sentences, reliance on 'doing' words (nouns and verbs), avoidance of 'descriptive' ones (adjectives or adverbs), and a detached, matter-of-fact portrayal of human suffering – most striking in his clinically colloquial depiction of a 'woman having a kid' – characterized a writer whose un-showy style, at its best, gained power from its lack of sentiment. In this respect, Hemingway arguably came closer than many of his author-journalist peers and contemporaries to embodying the 'strict' definition of a *reporter* – by stripping his writing of all traces of personal opinion or emotion. Contrast this with

In Cold Blood (1966), Truman Capote's career-defining but (latterly) contentious 'non-fiction novel' forensically examining the brutal murders of a family of farmers and the ensuing police investigation. In a passage (typical of the book's style) in which Capote describes the traumatic experience of labourers tasked with burning the victims' possessions, he liberally injects flashes of colour and description, in an effort to tug at the proverbial heart-strings. In it, Capote describes how the men first drove deep into a field 'the shimmering tawny yellow of November', before building 'a pyramid of Nancy's pillows, the bedclothes, the mattresses, the playroom couch' and setting fire to it, in the presence of a close family friend, the 'gentle, genially dignified' Andy Erhart, with his 'work-calloused hands and sunburned neck'.

'Shimmering tawny yellow', 'genially dignified', 'work-calloused' – none of these adjectival phrases would have any place in the works of Hemingway. The richness of Capote's descriptive prose and the quality of his insights allow his reporting to 'breathe' and convey a depth of understanding of the characters and places he encounters that is not only wholly absent in most routine news accounts but remains underexplored in Hemingway's calculatedly 'distant' hands. In all other respects, though, Capote retains a reportorial style, skilfully treading the fine journalistic line between observer and commentator. This was a talent he would use to 'define' reportage in the eyes of many, as a regular contributor to the *New Yorker* – the publication that brought him his widest audience.

From 'Gonzo' to 'New' Journalism – The Evolution of Reportage, American-style

During the late 1960s and early 1970s, reportage came of age in a particularly colourful way in the United States. Inspired by the beat poets, their chosen leisure drugs (principally LSD), and a free-spirited, counter-cultural ethos, a new generation of 'Gonzo' journalists emerged (the obscure term is an amalgamation of bastardized linguistic elements that came to refer to an unashamedly subjective and opinionated approach to reporting). Gonzo journalists made it their mission to document, through personal *experience*, the alternative lifestyles increasingly being embraced by those disaffected with the slow demise of the 'American Dream'. Among the foremost practitioners of Gonzo reportage was Hunter S. Thompson, the writer of *Fear and Loathing in Las Vegas*. Although Thompson's most famous and quotable work is the drug-addled self-portrait he paints in *Fear and Loathing* (like *Down and Out* and *In Cold Blood*, a book-length example of literary journalism with all the appearance of a novel), his reportage is often at its best when he is exploring a less familiar sub-culture. Nowhere does he do so more vividly than in *Hell's Angels: A Strange and Terrible Saga*, his 1966 experiential investigation into America's then-favourite folk-devils: the sometimes Satanic, often savage, invariably sexually voracious motorcycling gangs of the title. Through a mixture of textual analysis of everything from news reports to Hollywood screenplays and his own first-hand ethnographic encounters with the 'Angels', Thompson skilfully exposes their excesses while simultaneously debunking the popular hysteria that would have them perceived as latter-day Vikings, raping and pillaging their way around the United States. The following passage is typical of the technique he employs throughout to 'show' rather than 'tell' his readers about the nature of the Angels' lifestyle. Like the 'New Journalists' who followed him, Thompson was not afraid of using the first person and bringing himself into his writing when the need arose. But his prose was at its most effective when he found a way of combining this experiential approach with chunks of dialogue and straight reportage in which his subjects 'narrativized' their thoughts, actions, anecdotes and opinions in their own words, as illustrated here:

A run is a lot of things to the Angels: a party, an exhibition, and an exercise in solidarity. 'You never know how many Angels there are until you go on a big run,' says Zorro. 'Some get snuffed, some drop out, some go to the slammer and there's always new guys who've joined. That's why the runs are important – you find out who's on your side.'

It takes a strong leader like Barger to maintain the discipline necessary to get a large group of Angels to the run's destination. Trouble can break out almost anywhere. (The Angels won't admit it but one of the main kicks they get on a run comes from spooking and jangling citizens on the way.) They'd have no problem getting from the Bay Area to Bass Lake if they wanted to travel incognito, dressed like other weekenders and riding in Fords or Chevrolets. But this is out of the question. They wear their party clothes, making themselves as conspicuous as possible.

'People are already down on us because we're Hell's Angels,' Zorro explained. 'This is why we like to blow their minds. It just more or less burns 'em, that's all. They hate anything that's not right for their way of living.'

Here *Hell's Angels* becomes as much social anthropology as journalism: a picaresque travelogue that acts as the perfect antidote to the lurid claims made about the 'big ugly street fighters', with their 'swinging chains and big wrenches', by journalists, judges, police and politicians.

The other most influential 'Gonzo' journalist beside Thompson was arguably Tom Wolfe. Perhaps best known as the author of the satirical 1980s novel, *The Bonfire of the Vanities*, two decades earlier Wolfe had introduced the world to what came to be known as 'New Journalism' in *The Electric Kool Aid Acid Test* (1968), his bestselling literary road movie chronicling the LSD-fuelled misadventures of fellow journalist-turned-novelist Ken Kesey, writer of *One Flew over the Cuckoo's Nest*. While Wolfe's encounters with Kesey's 'Pranksters' were (like Thompson's with his bikers) rendered in a form fusing first-person observation with his subjects' own accounts, his style was arguably more playful, experimental and, in its use of impressionistic language, overtly novel-like than Thompson's. In one memorable passage, he described how the pranksters' lurid transport, a psychedelic bus festooned with American flags and 'blaring rock'n'roll', blazed a trail through the 'twisty green Gothic' grounds of a 'great gingerbread mansion' – likening the incongruous audacious spectacle to a 'rolling yahooing circus'.

It should probably come as no surprise that 'Gonzo' and 'New' journalism were not to everyone's tastes. When Thompson, Wolfe and their fellow mavericks first unleashed their extraordinary run of riotous, if wilfully undisciplined, works on an unsuspecting (and ill-prepared) public, the initial reaction from proponents of traditional journalism was one of outrage. In one scathing 13,000-word diatribe published in the *New York Review of Books*, cultural critic Dwight Macdonald dismissed Wolfe and his compatriots as 'parajournalists' who had committed the cardinal sin of supplanting 'information' – in his view, the principle component of true journalism – with 'misinformation', 'non-facts' and (horror of horrors) 'entertainment'. That such an esteemed, occasionally self-important, publication was prepared to dedicate so much space – and intellectual energy – to criticizing journalism's new literary turn, however, was a mark of how seriously it was being taken. It is hardly surprising, then, that both 'Gonzo' and 'New' journalism continue to exert such an influence – inspiring so many budding reporters and feature-writers in the process.

Crusading Reportage

Aside from 'literary' journalism, there is one other great reportorial tradition that owes a large debt to reportage. This is the strand of immersive investigative reporting commonly known as 'crusading' or 'campaigning' journalism. Among the most noted practitioners of this form are veteran Middle-East correspondent Robert Fisk, a mainstay of Britain's *Independent* newspaper, the late Paul Foot, and the equally left-wing Australian journalist John Pilger, whose prolific writings have included exhaustive dispatches from under-reported conflict zones ranging from Kosovo to East Timor to the Sudan.

Reportage of this kind, however, has a long genealogy. Investigative journalism relying on experiential eyewitness and, where necessary, undercover testimony researched 'in the field', often over lengthy periods, has a proud tradition stretching back to the late nineteenth and early twentieth centuries. Back then, pioneers like Joseph Pulitzer – the newspaper magnate whose enduring legacy is the eponymous prize still regarded as the most prestigious annual journalism award – actively encouraged their reporters to give voice to the voiceless (women, the poor, the mentally ill) and, as and when justified, discomfort the powerful. These early 'muckrakers' (a term coined not as an insult but a compliment by then US president Theodore Roosevelt) included a number of female journalists – perhaps unsurprisingly, given that one of the most burning social issues of the time was the emasculation of women. Of these, Nellie Bly was perhaps the most fearless and accomplished, her most daring exposé (and her first professional assignment) being an undercover investigation into the systematic physical and psychological abuse meted out to mental patients at Blackwell's Island asylum – an institution to which she was able to gain access only by faking her own insanity. This short extract from Chapter 13 of Bly's resulting *Ten Days in a Mad-House* (1887) (originally titled *Choking and Beating Patients*) typifies the at-times visceral imagery she used to convey the harsh regime she witnessed there:

Soon after my advent a girl called Urena Little-Page was brought in. She was, as she had been born, silly, and her tender spot was, as with many sensible women, her age. She claimed eighteen, and would grow very angry if told to the contrary. The nurses were not long in finding this out, and then they teased her.

'Urena,' said Miss Grady, 'the doctors say that you are thirty-three instead of eighteen,' and the other nurses laughed. They kept up this until the simple creature began to yell and cry, saying she wanted to go home and that everybody treated her badly. After they had gotten all the amusement out of her they wanted and she was crying, they began to scold and tell her to keep quiet. She grew more hysterical every moment until they pounced upon her and slapped her face and knocked her head in a lively fashion. This made the poor creature cry the more, and so they choked her. Yes, actually choked her. Then they dragged her out to the closet, and I heard her terrified cries hush into smothered ones. After several hours' absence she returned to the sitting-room, and I plainly saw the marks of their fingers on her throat for the entire day.

Decades later, the Vietnam War was to provide the backdrop for one of the most venerated pieces of extended investigative reporting of all time. In *My Lai 4: A Report on the Massacre and its Aftermath* (1969), legendary reporter Seymour Hersh documents, in often-obsessive detail, his dogged year-long pursuit of the full picture behind a tiny press agency item referring to the then-upcoming court martial of one Lieutenant William Calley for the unlawful killing of 109 'Oriental human beings'. The book was the outcome of an investigation which took Hersh on a 50,000-mile odyssey, crisscrossing America, to track down and interview fifty members of Charlie Company – the battalion responsible for the bloodshed. In so doing, he uncovered what has since become one of the most notorious establishment conspiracies of modern times: an attempt to 'hush up' the coordinated 1968 mass murder by US soldiers of some 500 North Vietnamese civilians in the village of My Lai.

While respecting many of its traditions, Hersh's classic plays havoc with the 'rules' of conventional reportage: encounters with those he interviews personally are rendered with the clarity of first-hand experience, but he describes equally vividly (as if watching from nearby) scenes of carnage conjured up by their testimony that he can only have 'witnessed' vicariously. In this respect, Hersh's writings on My Lai were to act as templates for any number of wildly different, but equally accomplished, examples of book-length reportage, from *Hungry for Home*, Cole Moreton's lyrical history of the 1953 flight of the last inhabitants of Ireland's Blasket archipelago, to *Guardian* feature-writer Andy Beckett's meticulously researched *When the Lights Went Out*, which offers an unashamedly revisionist perspective on the political conflicts, industrial unrest and energy blackouts of 1970s Britain – historical events he (like Moreton, but unlike Hersh) was too young himself to remember.

Given its subject matter, it is hardly surprising that Hersh's (quite literally) blow-by-blow account makes for harrowing reading. Hersh knowingly uses a clipped, unfussy prose style to convey the unfeeling, mechanical way in which the soldiers moved around the village, coldly dispatching its occupants. Their actions are rendered all the more shocking by the quotes he intersperses from his interviewees, documenting the robotic way the troops dispatched their victims, many of them children, in defiance of their vain pleas for mercy.

Like all the finest examples of reportage, including most of those cited here, Hersh's account is a work whose legacy continues to be felt well beyond the confines of the narrow realm of journalism decades after the events it describes.

5. THE JOURNALISTIC ESSAY

THERE IS ONE TYPE of 'long-form' journalism to which we have, as yet, paid scant attention. This is the journalistic essay – a somewhat more rarefied and meditative form of writing which, while it may draw on some of the stylistic tropes familiar from our discussion of features and reportage, is in other respects distinct. In particular, where reportage and longer, more colourful, feature articles tend to adopt the language and conventions of *literature*, the essay (as its name suggests) is often more closely indebted to the prose style of *academic* argument and criticism. Moreover, most journalistic essays, like scholarly ones, are framed around a central 'case' or 'thesis' – normally (by dint of appearing in a journalistic publication) about a topical debate or issue. Like obituaries, therefore, they are often written not by 'jobbing hacks' but historians, scientists, lawyers, politicians, members of the clergy and other assorted 'experts' commissioned to pen them on a freelance basis. In short, essays tend to be left to those regarded as best placed to comment on a subject with *authority*.

It seems appropriate, then, to include a short chapter on the journalistic essay at this stage – sandwiched, as we are, between several chapters focusing on the main forms of 'factual' journalism and a switch of emphasis to looking at more opinionated types of article.

The Rise of the 'Essayists' and their Place in Popular Journalism

By their nature, journalistic essays tend to be analytical, hypothetical and of considerable length. Unlike news stories, features, most profiles and even reviews, essays are generally exempted from the customary journalistic rule of thumb that requires the writer to produce some evidence of primary research. The nature of the essay, like those written by under-graduate and postgraduate university students, is that it relies not on interviews or other forms of traditional journalistic 'legwork', but rather on knowledge acquired through background reading and study, and intellectual qualities like logic and reason. For this reason alone, its natural 'home' has traditionally been the pages of the broadsheet newspaper, the culture or features section/supplement, or the 'highbrow' literary or political periodical.

H.G. Wells, novelist, science-fiction visionary and prolific essayist, was always keen to debunk any suggestion that there was an 'art' (let alone a science) to constructing essays. In *The Writing of Essays*, published in 1897, he claimed essay-writing could be learnt 'in a brief ten minutes or so', and described it as 'so simple, so entirely free from canons of criticism, and withal so delightful, that one must needs wonder why all men are not essayists'. Nonetheless, later on in the same piece he came as close as anyone has ever managed to pinpointing a 'formula' for how best to draw readers in to an essay – a task which, after all, is incumbent on any long-form journalist, as they try to entice people to invest time and energy in reading and absorbing a piece that requires considerable patience to plough through from start to finish. 'An abrupt beginning is much admired, after the fashion of the clown's entrance through the chemist's window', he mused, adding that the writer should then 'whack at your reader at once, hit him over the head with the sausages, brisk him up with the poker, bundle him into the wheelbarrow, and so carry him away with you before he knows where you are.'

Sage advice indeed – and all the more so for the fact that

Wells might just as easily have been ruminating on the role of the feature- or profile-writer, or even the canny reporter who teases his readers with a puzzling or ambiguous opening paragraph before hitting them with the punchline of his carefully honed dropped intro. Given the inherent playfulness of this approach, it is hardly surprising that, as with reportage, journalistic essay-writing has attracted more than its fair share of novelists. Laurie Lee, W. Somerset Maugham, Aldous Huxley, Graham Greene and, of course, George Orwell were all keen essayists. But among those most accomplished in the art of surprising and ensnaring readers in the vein Wells describes so eloquently was an earlier journalist-turned-author, Charles Dickens, who became highly adept at encapsulating his thoughts in concise, letter-like, 'short-form' essays he wrote for various publications, including *The Examiner* and his own magazine, *Household Words*. The following extract is taken from his treatise on a then-pioneering school project set up by philanthropists to educate poor children, written for the *Daily News*, the short-lived Liberal Party-supporting newspaper he set up in the 1840s to rival the Tory-leaning *Times:*

I offer no apology for entreating the attention of the readers of *The Daily News* to an effort which has been making for some three years and a half, and which is making now, to introduce among the most miserable and neglected outcasts in London, some knowledge of the commonest principles of morality and religion; to commence their recognition as immortal human creatures, before the Gaol Chaplain becomes their only schoolmaster; to suggest to Society that its duty to this wretched throng, foredoomed to crime and punishment, rightfully begins at some distance from the police office; and that the careless maintenance from year to year, in this, the capital city of the world, of a vast hopeless nursery of ignorance, misery and vice; a breeding place for the hulks and jails: is horrible to contemplate.

(Charles Dickens, 'Crime and Education', *Daily News,*
September 1843)

For all the lessons we can draw from such examples, the world inhabited by Greene and Orwell, let alone Dickens and his like, seems very distant today. Given the mass media's oft-criticized preference for soap opera-style rows between politicians and celebrities over serious debate about policies and issues, surely the journalistic essay must be a dying breed – a casualty of changing public appetites in an era of dwindling leisure-time and push-button access to handily packaged, bite-sized chunks of digital infotainment? And why wade through someone's 5,000-word reflection (however erudite and incisive) on a film or book you can view or buy yourself with the press of a key or swipe of a screen, let alone the life and times of a historical figure, event or movement you can bone up on in a few short minutes by skimming its entry on Wikipedia?

In truth, though, for all the demands it places on readers to concentrate and consider, the journalistic essay has proved a surprisingly resilient staple of even relatively 'mass-market' publications – despite the vicissitudes of our rapidly evolving media environment. If authored by someone with demonstrable knowledge and credibility – and with a strong enough 'thesis' to argue – the essay can be a highly effective way of exploring a complex and contested subject and persuading readers to spend time thinking about it, too. Take the following example by the late cultural theorist Richard Hoggart. Published in the then-weekly 'Saturday Essay' slot in *The Independent*, the 1998 article relates to a then-simmering public debate about the nature of English (and British) identity:

> LONG AGO, at school, we used to write on the front of our exercise books our names and then: Hunslet, Leeds, Yorkshire, England, Great Britain, The World, The Universe. We knew what we were and where we were; incidentally, hardly anyone included Europe.
>
> In America for a year, our young son, at four years old, looked up after a few weeks and said: 'I'm English, and I ought to be in England.' He too knew what and where.
>
> (Simon Hoggart, 'What does it mean to be English today?'
> *The Independent*, 5 September 1998)

Like any skilled essayist, Hoggart (an academic highly prac-
tised in the art) unfurls his carpet a bit at a time, but it is his
abrupt shift from recalling his and his son's attitudes in the past
towards reflecting on his thinking today that allows the article
to segue neatly into a wider consideration of how 'outsiders'
(non-Britons) perceive the British cultural identity crisis:

> Now, in old age, I am usually not quite sure what I am and, in
> particular, whether I wish to be 'British' or 'English', or both.
> No wonder foreigners are often confused or sniffy about our
> various nomenclatures. They don't usually relate 'Briton' to
> the early Britons. Many Americans think that 'Great Britain'
> is a typical boast instead of, in the 1707 Act of Union, an
> invention, what Defoe called 'A union of policy, not of affec-
> tions' (as Linda Colley recalls in her admirable *Britons*).

So what was the 'excuse' for this essay – or, to use the correct
journalistic jargon, its 'peg'? To put Hoggart's arguments in their
correct historical context: at the time he was writing, Scotland,
Wales and Northern Ireland had just voted for devolution:
the transfer of constitutional power from the Westminster
Parliament to their own, self-determining assemblies. There
was putative talk about the possibility of similar bodies being
set up in the English regions. And, barely a year earlier, Sir
James Goldsmith's anti-European Union Referendum Party
had made (often fatal) inroads into the majorities of a number
of 'Europhile' Conservative MPs as they struggled to hold on to
their parliamentary seats in the face of New Labour's relentless
assault in the 1997 general election. In essence, while there may
have been no one *immediate* 'event' to merit a more straightforward journalistic article at that time – a feature, let alone a news
story – there were more than enough *cumulative* developments,
or strands, to justify a more reflective, speculative and provocative 'think piece' of this kind.

Another, still relatively common, form of journalistic essay to
be found in mainstream publications is what we might term the
'expert opinion piece'. Chapter 6 explores opinion *columns* – the
regular articles or pages penned by newspapers' and magazines'

own 'in-house' comment writers – so we will confine ourselves here to the breed of longer-form articles that tend to be the preserve of experts in their fields, rather than career journalists. To take one example, expert-authored essays on literary subjects have long been a mainstay of *The Guardian's* Saturday 'Review' section, with established authors holding forth, often in great detail, on all manner of subjects close to their hearts – from the role of the heroine in Victorian fiction to the works of an individual novelist or the merits and pitfalls of a particular genre. The following extract comes from a 2007 essay by Giles Foden, author of *The Last King of Scotland*, who uses it to ruminate on the enduring reputation of Joseph Conrad as both a literary giant and a writer of page-turning, if existentialist, action-adventure novels. Foden's thesis, timed to mark the 150th anniversary of Conrad's death (and to promote his own public discussion of *The Secret Agent* with fellow author Iain Sinclair later the same week), is that today's digitally interconnected, yet socially atomized, global society has much to learn from the deep sense of moral optimism he identifies in Conrad's writing:

> As Conrad put it in his 1905 essay 'Books': 'To be hopeful in an artistic sense it is not necessary to think that the world is good. It is enough to believe that there is no impossibility of it being made so.'
> This shouldn't be taken as the defensive, hollowed-out position it appears to be. Positively, usefully, a sense of relativism-as-virtue was what Conrad was all about. It was what he valued. On the 150th anniversary of his birth and the centenary of the publication of *The Secret Agent*, such a value seems worth exploring again.
>
> (Giles Foden, 'The moral agent', *The Guardian*, 1 December 2007)

Like many other essays of its kind, this article breaks numerous journalistic taboos. Far from couching his arguments in plain English (a subject to which we return in Chapter 11), Foden casts aside the newspaper-style book by littering his prose with often-esoteric scholarly language. But a refusal to 'talk down' to readers – by contrast, an expectation that they will 'think up' – is par for the course in journalistic essay-writing, and those essays that appear in the sections and supplements of broadsheet papers, and more thoughtful consumer magazines, are no exception to this rule.

Essays for Specialist Audiences

While essays may be a diminishing, if not wholly endangered, species in mainstream publications, they remain far more commonplace in certain specialist journals – particularly those focusing on the worlds of politics, economics, literature and the arts. From weekly magazines like *The Spectator* and the *New Statesman* to highbrow monthly current affairs magazines like *The Economist* and *Intelligent Life* to bookish periodicals like the *London Magazine* and the *Times Literary Supplement*, there remain a number of 'showpiece' journalistic platforms available to the foremost thinkers of the day to dispense their wisdom in essay form. Take the following extract from an essay by the philosopher A.C. Grayling that appeared in an extensive supplement on the subject of poverty published by *Prospect* magazine: a monthly focusing on a mix of British politics, world affairs and culture that is unapologetically aimed at an educated, middle-class, liberal audience. In it, he reflects on various definitions of the concept of poverty, and makes the case that members of developed societies have a collective duty to work to eradicate both relative and absolute forms of material want as a matter of basic 'social justice'. As with Hoggart's essay on Britishness and Englishness, there were any number of 'pegs', and plenty of background context, to justify Grayling's piece: among other things, numerous studies by non-government organizations (NGOs) and United Nations bodies highlighting the growing gulf between rich and poor nations, and (back home in Britain) the then-Coalition government's blizzard of measures to cut social security benefits and make qualification criteria tougher, and rising demand for 'food banks' among those unable to afford basic family essentials. However, as befits an essay published in a less mainstream title (and written by a philosopher), Grayling's approach to his subject is not to name-check any particular politician, party or even country, let alone to root his essay, explicitly, in the 'here and now' of a topical social or economic trend. Instead, aided by an accompanying photograph of a boarded-up street in Salford, Greater Manchester, he *assumes* his audience is already aware of the broad premise underlying his article. He then uses this (unwritten) premise as a spring-board to launch into an often elliptical discussion, whose most notable quotation comes from nineteenth-century diarist Dr Samuel Johnson:

> Dr Johnson wrote, 'Slow rises worth, by poverty depressed.' Both absolute and relative poverty represent a loss of human potential, in the specific sense of a loss of the contribution that people can make if given a chance to apply themselves in some sphere. In the case of someone starving in a refugee camp during an African drought, the point is obvious enough. But relative poverty can mean that an individual is unable to afford suitable clothes for an interview, or the train fare to where the interview is held. Of course in more advanced countries efforts are made to help people in these circumstances with subsidies as part of welfare; but the point generalises. Talk of 'cycles of deprivation' is shorthand for an account of how the narrowness of opportunity for the relatively poor can persist down generations, perhaps getting worse with attrition of educational aspirations, and with them knowledge of what opportunities are on offer in life and work.

(A.C. Grayling, 'What is poverty?' *Prospect,* 19 November 2013)

Such conceits would be unthinkable in other types of long-form journalism: reportage, let alone the conventional feature, stops well short of allowing its writers the licence to pontificate in such an overtly cerebral and argumentative fashion. For the essayist, however, this licence goes with the territory, and is another mark of why the essay is a category of journalism worth considering in its own unique right.

6. THE OPINIONATED JOURNALIST

'DON'T PAY ANY ATTENTION to what they write about you. Just measure it in inches', Andy Warhol once remarked of that curious breed of journalists: critics. His words were, at once, a typically idiosyncratic variant of the old adage that 'no publicity is bad publicity' and an extension of the disdainful view attributed (largely erroneously) to any number of named artists, writers and performers that criticism is the preserve of 'those who can't *do*': self-anointed arbiters of popular opinion who have never made a record, directed a film or written a book themselves and, more to the point, would have no idea how to do so. Yet, however much bravado they might display as they profess not to read reviews or care what critics think of their work, in truth 'creatives' can be a thin-skinned bunch – just as well-judged, well-targeted criticism undoubtedly helps to inform, and at times sway, public opinion.

All the aforementioned truisms might just as easily be said of various other kinds of journalism that depart from the 'norm' of objectivity that is the basis for the types of writing explored in the first four chapters of this book. Whether in the guise of the lengthy essays examined in Chapter 5, newspaper leader columns and opinion-editorial (op-ed) pages, or the rash of comment-based web-logs (blogs) that have proliferated over the past fifteen years, there seem to be more opportunities than ever for journalists (amateurs and professionals alike) to air their personal views on everything from politics to sport to the arts.

Moreover, taken together with other recent journalistic trends – from the resurgence of first-person narratives in some forms of feature, especially in the United States, to the rise in popularity of the experiential consumer pieces outlined in Chapter 2 – there is a case to be made that the increasing 'norm' of early twenty-first-century journalism is the jettisoning of any pretend objectivity in favour of a more honestly *subjective* approach which instead creates space for the journalist to air his/her own views. In the sections that follow, we look at the three main forms taken by openly opinionated journalism in the print and online media: reviews, leaders and op-ed pieces, and comment-based blogs.

The Art of Critical Reviewing

The terms 'review' and 'criticism' are normally used to describe articles focusing on the appreciation of what might broadly be bracketed as 'works of art', whether those works be paintings, novels, poems, performances or any other art *form*. However, while the terms 'reviewer' and 'critic' are treated as being more or less interchangeable in journalistic circles, the use of the word *criticism* is generally reserved for the more studiedly analytical and argumentative 'reviews' to be found in academic journals, as opposed to newspapers, magazines or other (more mainstream) publications. As this is a book about journalistic writing, as opposed to scholarship, the types of review-writing and criticism referred to here will predominantly be of the latter kind.

Notwithstanding our focus on 'popular' forms of criticism, though, it is worth discriminating at the outset between what might be described as the (jobbing) reviewer and the (more expert) *critic* – if nothing else, to emphasize the fact that, even within the narrow realm of journalism, there are such things as 'good' and 'bad' reviews. 'Reviewers are lazy; critics are not', was the blunt assessment of the late Anthony Burgess, who managed to find time to pen numerous book reviews for regional and national newspapers when not producing his prolific output of novels and screenplays. Though knowingly provocative, Burgess had a point. It has long been the case, in the provincial press especially, that many day-to-day reviews – whether of pop concerts or new film releases – are written not by dedicated, paid reviewers hired because they are genuine aficionados in those fields but by reporters or feature-writers who are tasked with filing them on top of their 'day jobs' for the price of a free ticket and a reserved seat at the opening night. Even national newspapers and specialist arts magazines employ very few full-time arts writers, and this can lead to an over-reliance on generalist, commission-chasing freelancers and enthusiastic amateurs over specialist critics. By contrast, the few fortunate individuals who manage to claw their way into the handful of hallowed in-house literary editor positions will tend (by dint of the competition for such posts) to be much more experienced and, therefore, knowledgeable. As Burgess went on to explain, specifically in relation to book criticism:

> The status and, indeed, physical condition of the reviewer is summed up in a trenchant article by George Orwell. The man looks older than he is. He sits at a table covered with rubbish which he dare not disturb, for there may be a small cheque lying under it.
>
> He began his sub-literary career as a genuinely literary one, with high hopes, noble aspirations. But he has sunk to the condition of a hack. He has learnt the trick of reviewing anything, including books he has no hope of understanding.
>
> (Anthony Burgess, 'Confessions of the hack trade', *The Guardian*, 4 March 2012)

What, then, is the recipe for a 'good' review, and how should one set about writing one? There are arguably four key qualities that distinguish more effective, insightful reviews from those that are less so. Firstly, a review should contain sufficient colour and description to 'bring to life' whatever is being reviewed and make it *meaningful* to the reader: describing a live performance as 'amazing' or 'impressive' actually tells us very little about its qualities, and it *tells* us so little because it fails to *show* us precisely what the event looked, sounded and felt like to watch/ hear/attend in person. Even before it gets into the business of explaining the 'who, what, where, when, how, why' elements of the performance itself, though, the review first needs to tick another box: by filling us in (if only briefly) with the back-story or context that is necessary for us to appreciate its *newsworthiness*. If, for example, this was the first live gig performed by a once-popular singer or band for decades – or their first public appearance following a major personal drama or change of artistic direction – then the 'peg' for the review is suddenly made clearer, and what follows in terms of criticism is likely to make more sense. Next, the review must, in the end, give us a sense of what the writer thought about the performance (or book, film, CD etc.): in other words, whether he or she judged it to be any good, and if not, why not. The folly of using the first person for review-writing will be addressed in Chapter 10, but for now it is worth stressing that there is no value in a review that leaves the reader with no clear idea at the end of it whether it is likely to be worth their time (and money) watching that film, reading that book, or hanging on the premium-rate line queuing to buy that concert ticket. Last but not least, reviews – like news stories – tend to follow a set structure, which distinguishes them from the various longer forms of journalism we have explored since Chapter 1. As this underlying structure determines where other components fit into the jigsaw, it is to this we will now turn.

'Sandwiches', 'Burgers' and the Art of Saying Just Enough – But Not Too Much

Where news stories follow an 'inverted triangle/pyramid' formula – foregrounding all the juiciest information at the top and leaving the least vital details to the end, from where they can safely be edited out if necessary – most reviews adopt a structure which places as much emphasis on their closing as their opening (or intervening) paragraphs. In the case of film, theatre and many book reviews, this structure is often referred to as the 'burger' or 'sandwich' approach, as illustrated by

Figure 6.1. While the central 'filling' pores over the key details of the performance or product being reviewed, it is sandwiched between two halves of a bun (or slices of bread, if you will) that contain, respectively, the context and evaluation that between them constitute the review itself. To be more precise, the top 'slice' is used to set the scene with the relevant context or background that gives some justification for the newsworthiness of the item being reviewed – for example, the fact that this new horror movie represents a departure for its director, whose previous films have all been aimed at children, or that his last release was met with scathing (or adoring) reviews. The 'filling' will tend to be the shortest, most descriptive section. Here the writer will usually introduce the main protagonists of the film, play or novel and give readers a brief outline of its premise and/or key themes, while taking care not to reveal any key plot twists, or 'spoilers'. Finally, the bottom 'slice' should be the most substantial part of the article, and the one that contains the most analysis and criticism. In it, the reviewer should 'lay his cards on the table' – giving his considered assessment of the strengths and weaknesses of the work and (as in all good examples of critical writing, from opinion columns to academic essays) supporting his judgements with reasoned argument backed by *evidence*. It is here that reviewers often explicitly 'rate' work, too – for instance, by awarding it stars or a score out of ten.

Though the sandwich/burger structure is the default option for reviews of films, books, plays, musicals, opera, ballet and, to some extent, albums – in essence, artistic products that have a central plot or 'narrative' to make up the 'filling' – it is less often used by reviewers of art exhibitions, music concerts and other types of performance, such as dance or physical theatre. In these circumstances, critics (often highly knowledgeable subject specialists) may employ any number of more imaginative approaches, tailoring them very closely to the niche audiences for whom they are writing.

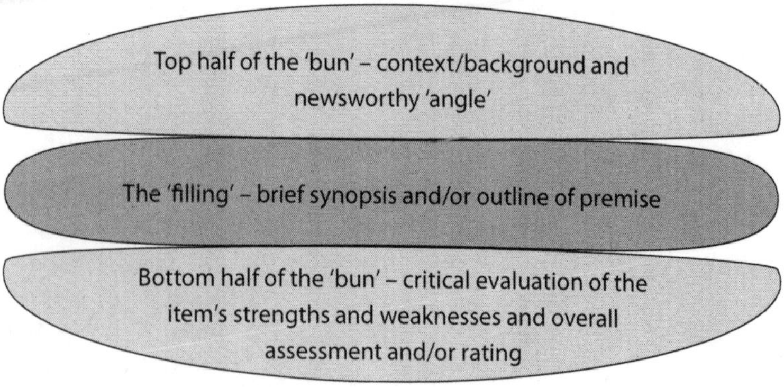

Top half of the 'bun' – context/background and
newsworthy 'angle'

The 'filling' – brief synopsis and/or outline of premise

Bottom half of the 'bun' – critical evaluation of the
item's strengths and weaknesses and overall
assessment and/or rating

Figure 6.1

The Top Half of the 'Bun' by Example – Some Common Ingredients

If there is one component of a review which bears any resemblance to a news story it is the top half of the burger bun, in which the writer will effectively foreground what he or she considers to be the topic's main 'peg': in other words, the reason why readers of this particular publication should be interested in this particular new piece of work, by this particular artist, at this particular time. The short extract that follows offers a model example of this approach. In it, *Independent* literary editor Boyd Tonkin sets the scene for a lengthy review of a new book by little-known (in Britain) writer Mircea Cartarescu, by tying in his latest work to a then-febrile tabloid debate about the risk of a flood of migrants from his native Romania entering the UK following an impending relaxation of European Union migration rules:

> The media hysterics who depict Romania solely as the home of demon migrant hordes will not care that a novelist from that country became a hot tip for the Nobel Prize in Literature this year.

> (Boyd Tonkin, 'Blinding: The Left Wing, by Mircea Cartaerscu:
> Book review – memory and satire meld magically in this Bucharest
> tale', *The Independent*, 28 November 2013)

An alternative approach, but one designed to achieve the same ends – hooking readers by signalling to them what is innately 'newsworthy' about its subject – is this from the late Kenneth Tynan, one-time doyen of theatre criticism. In opening his review for *The Observer* of now-classic musical satire *Oh, What a Lovely War!*, Tynan chose to dwell less on the play itself than the mastermind behind it: the renowned impresario Joan Littlewood, whose every production was, at the time, eagerly awaited:

> It seems to me quite likely that when the annals of our theatre in the middle years of the twentieth century come to be written, one name will lead all the rest: that of Joan Littlewood. Others write plays, direct them or act in them: Miss Littlewood alone 'makes theatre'.
>
> She has come back to Theatre Workshop, after two years' lamented absence, with a triumph unimaginable anywhere but on a stage; it belongs uniquely to its birthplace – the bare boards that are Littlewood's home ground, filled with the passion of Littlewood's home team.
>
> (Tynan, 'Littlewood returns in triumph', *The Observer*, 24 March 1963)

While there may be no strict 'right or wrong' way of framing a given review, as with news stories there is usually a broad measure of agreement between critics on rival publications over what is most 'newsworthy' (for good or ill) about a given product or performance – or the artist or artists responsible for it. Differences in house style notwithstanding, the first new recording released by a reclusive rock star in twenty-five years is liable to be approached from the same broad 'intro angle' whichever publication it appears in – whether the *Daily Express*, *The Guardian* or *NME*. Take the following two examples – both opening paragraphs (or top slices) from reviews of *The Next Day*, the first studio album by David Bowie in more than a decade, which was suddenly released on an unsuspecting public in early 2013.

To take these two publications in order, the mid-market

tabloid adopts perhaps the most 'rule-bending' approach to framing its intro – by using the 'royal we' (almost as much of a no-no as the first person). In all other respects, though, it obeys the maxim that Bowie's prolonged absence from the music scene should be seen as the yardstick by which the quality of his latest CD should be judged:

> WE could just fill this review with superlatives hailing the fascinating genius of one of the world's most influential artists and conveniently ignore any critical musings on the album, his first in 10 years.
>
> (Stephen Unwin, 'CD review: Bowie – The Next Day, *Daily Express*, 8 March 2013)

In a musically literate, if drawn-out, intro, *The Guardian's* multi award-winning Alexis Petridis crafts a neat summation of all the factors that make the release an 'event' that reads like a mini-essay in itself. The article begins with a provocative tease, as if suggesting the hype surrounding the album might be ill-founded:

> When David Bowie chose to break a decade's silence by releasing a single, Where Are We Now?, on his 66th birthday, dissenting voices were hard to find amid the clamour made by people eager to welcome him back. Some argued that the clamour was part of the problem: it drowned out the music, which perhaps wasn't worthy of the noisy excitement it had caused.
>
> (Alex Petridis, 'David Bowie: The Next Day – review', *The Guardian*, 25 February 2013)

It is not long before he is easing towards his 'punchline', though – weaving in erudite references to earlier Bowie classics to nudge us towards the conclusion that, however much the naysayers might have a point, this comeback record is worthy of serious appreciation. This will set the tone (and theme) for the rest of the piece, which ends with the album's being awarded four out of a maximum five stars, in recognition of its musical quality:

The reason people were so thrilled Bowie was back, they suggested, was founded in the music he made in the 1970s, a decade when almost every new album he released was an astonishingly sure-footed leap forward into uncharted territory. But *Where Are We Now?* was no *Heroes* or *Sound and Vision.* Rather, it was a charming, fragile ballad.

(Ibid.)

Though written for contrasting newspapers, with very different target readerships, both intros mention the same essential facts in order to underline the newsworthiness of the subject being reviewed. In so doing, they implicitly 'justify' the space reserved for the article – a key function of the top half of the bun, as it seeks to lure readers into setting aside the time to read it.

Filling in the Gaps: the 'Meat' of the Article

If the filling of a review (often its shortest section) has one key function it is to provide sufficient detail about the *substance* of an artwork to persuade readers to want to view, hear or otherwise experience it themselves – or, alternatively, deter them from wasting their time doing so. In the context of a film, novel or play, there needs to be just enough information provided to whet the reader's appetite (or turn them off) but not so much that, by the time they finish reading, there is little need for them to bother either way, because the whole plot has been revealed or the surprise denouement ruined. The following example demonstrates how *not* to fill your burger or sandwich. Taken from the *Daily Telegraph*'s review of the film *Never Let Me Go*, based on the novel of the same name by Booker Prize-winning author Kazuo Ishiguro, it makes the cardinal error of revealing the film's central plot twist. This is the fact that its main protagonists, a group of 'orphaned' boarding-school pupils, are in fact clones being bred to sacrifice their body parts in the cause of human transplant surgery. Rather than teasing his audience, as he might have done, with the promise of a sinister, but unspecified, purpose behind the children's closeted upbringing,

111

critic Tim Robey writes:

> Carey Mulligan narrates as Kathy H, a diligent and demure student at Hailsham, the school whose pupils realise they're something special.
> The script isn't coy about this — they're clones, being reared for their organs.

(Tim Robey, 'Never Let Me Go, review', Daily Telegraph, 10 February 2011)

Another weakness of some film reviews is the critic's lack of acknowledgement – or, in some cases, apparent lack of *awareness* – of a movie's source material. While engagingly written in many respects, the following example, from a critique of the same film in the London-focused UK edition of global listings magazine *Time Out*, displays all the flaws of a review that is effectively criticizing the film's source material (Ishiguro's novel), rather than the movie itself:

> You wouldn't know it from the poster campaign. You couldn't guess it from the cast list. Even watching the film, the horrible reality is only gradually revealed. And yet it's true: *Never Let Me Go* is ... a sci-fi movie.
> If ever proof were needed that cultural snobbery is alive and well, it's right here. *Never Let Me Go* is a film so ashamed of its own genre trappings that it goes to extreme and illogical lengths to pretend they don't exist.

(Tom Huddlestone, 'Never Let Me Go', Time Out, 8 February 2011)

Although the critic does go on to mention (and praise) the novel, most of the criticisms he makes of director Mark Romanek's adaptation might just as easily have been made of the book – which, arguably, is equally 'guilty' of going to 'extreme and illogical lengths' to 'pretend' it is not science fiction. Contrast both Robey and Huddlestone's approaches with that of the *New York Times*, which, out of respect for the novel, as much as the screenplay, skilfully treads the fine line between dropping tantalizing hints about the nature of the children's predicament (and the children themselves) and giving the game away entirely. Although Manohla Dargis, the paper's chief film critic, reveals one aspect of their macabre destiny early on – describing how they spend their early lives 'playing, quarrelling, forming friendships, while also receiving peculiar instruction about their ghastly future as organ donators' – she is careful not to undermine the efforts made both by Ishiguro and Romanek to keep audiences guessing about *precisely* what is going on, by only gradually unravelling the plot's multiple twists. Instead, Dargis emphasizes how 'like the children, you [viewers] initially have only a partial view of their lives, how they came to be at Hailsham and why, so that you learn with them' – adding that it would be 'unfair' to reveal more, because 'one of the pleasures of *Never Let Me Go*, on the page and on screen, comes from the detective work the story requires'. Significantly, the word 'clone' appears nowhere in her article.

Cutting to the Chase – the Bottom Half of the Bun

If the top half of the review bun has the task of catching the reader's eye and persuading them its subject is worthy of their attention, it is for the bottom half to serve up perhaps the article's most vital ingredient: the reviewer's verdict. This chunk tends to be longer, and more substantial, than either of the others, and significantly more so than the filling. Like a good feature, it will often return readers to a thought, theme or idea introduced in the opening section – creating a sense that the review is in some ways moving 'full circle' – but like a good *essay*, it will use examples and other 'evidence' to support the judgements it makes about the merits and weaknesses of what is being reviewed. A typical way the 'circular' approach works is for the critic to address any sense of expectation or anticipation set up in the opening section. In the case of the Bowie album, for example, many reviewers picked up the thread about this being the singer's first CD release for a decade, before addressing the question of whether the album was worth the wait and/or to what extent it bore comparison to the output of his critically acclaimed 1970s heyday (a perennial debate revived whenever this particular artist releases new material). Another tactic is for the reviewer to pick over the elements sketched in by the middle section: having introduced them in a purely *descriptive* way, he/she now faces having to evaluate how well the film or album hangs together as a whole; how accomplished the actors' or musicians' performances are; how poetic, dramatic or amusing the lyrics or dialogue are; and (perhaps above all else) how the work as a whole compares to other examples of its genre or pantheon and/or fits into the singer's/actor's/director's own personal oeuvre.

Meet the 'Opinion-formers': The Role of Op-ed Pieces and Leader Columns

Beyond the realm of artistic criticism, newspapers (and, to a lesser extent, magazines) conventionally reserve voicing their own opinions for one other key aspect of life: politics. Comment articles traditionally take one of two principal forms. Firstly, there is the leader column or editor's letter – effectively, the 'official mouthpiece' of the publication as a whole – in which a clear view is customarily expressed about a burning issue, or issues, of the day. Newspaper leaders are invariably 'un-authored', in that they do not carry by-lines. Instead, they are seen to act as the collective voice of the paper – for which read its editor or (in the eyes of some) proprietor. Leaders will also tend to address two or three subjects on a single day: typically, the main leader will focus on what the paper considers to be the most 'serious' issue of the day, while either or both of the (considerably shorter) second and third leaders will often tackle subjects that are more light-hearted, even frivolous. The magazine equivalents of leaders, meanwhile, are editor's letters. These are more informal, even conversational, pieces that tend to appear on pages three or four. As such, they are as much introductions to (or sales pitches for) the contents of the edition the reader has just opened as platforms for editors to hold forth on matters close to their, or their readerships', hearts.

In more 'serious' magazines, though – consumer titles focusing on politics, economics or culture, some of those catering for 'special-interest' audiences, or business-to-business ones aimed at particular professions or industries – the editor's letter can become as much a sounding-board for its author as a greetings card to its readers.

Secondly, there is the opinion piece. There will often be several of these in any given edition – each authored by a different named journalist, and focusing on a different topic (or topics). But whereas broadsheets will run a scattering of op-ed pieces on the same, or opposing, pages, tabloids usually allocate an entire page (or 'column') to each opinion-writer, scattering these throughout the paper. In addition, while broadsheet op-eds are generally written by professional journalists, tabloid columnists are as likely to be politicians, pundits, celebrities or those whose high-profile journalistic careers have elevated them to a measure of stardom.

Stating your Case without Sermonizing: The Art of the Leader

Anyone who has ever tried their hand at leader-writing will tell you it is not half as simple as it may look. While reporters and feature-writers have been known to hanker after the opportunity to drop their enforced objectivity, take a break from the often extensive legwork (interviews, unreturned phone calls, data-trawling and so forth) that goes into their articles, and instead air their own, unvarnished views on a subject, in truth there is much more to a good leader than initially meets the eye. For one thing, today's leaders (even those in broadsheets) tend to be fairly short and to-the-point: gone are the days when whole pages would be devoted to dense, highly analytical appraisals of every aspect of a thorny debate or issue. Like a good essay, moreover, the main leader needs to set out its stall in a logical, well-argued fashion, weaving in as much evidence as possible to support its position. The shorter leader items, too, may appear deceptively straightforward. While a disposable third leader item focusing on the latest passing fad in the world of show-business might not require many brain cells to digest, honing what often amounts to little more than a single sentence or paragraph into something punchy, witty and (even momentarily) diverting certainly does.

The following extract is from the opening salvo of *The Guardian's* main leader six days before the 2010 general election – traditionally a time when all, or most, papers state which party they are supporting in the coming contest, and occasionally urge their readers to do likewise. As the intro paragraphs indicate, this more than usually lengthy leader article was framed as an argument for change and, specifically, a justification for the paper's decision to switch allegiance from Labour to the Liberal Democrats, in so doing reviving its historic nineteenth-century 'liberal' tradition:

> Citizens have votes. Newspapers do not. However, if the *Guardian* had a vote in the 2010 general election it would be cast enthusiastically for the Liberal Democrats. It would be cast in the knowledge that not all the consequences are predictable, and that some in particular should be avoided. The vote would be cast with some important reservations and frustrations. Yet it would be cast for one great reason of principle above all.

> ('General election 2010: the liberal moment has come', *The Guardian*,
> 30 April 2010)

On this tantalizing note, the leader switches to a new paragraph – luring long-time readers onwards with the promise of resolving the mystery of its 'defection' from Labour:

> After the campaign that the Liberal Democrats have waged over this past month, for which considerable personal credit goes to Nick Clegg, the election presents the British people with a huge opportunity: the reform of the electoral system itself. Though Labour has enjoyed a deathbed conversion to aspects of the cause of reform, it is the Liberal Democrats who have most consistently argued that cause in the round

and who, after the exhaustion of the old politics, reflect and lead an overwhelming national mood for real change.

(Ibid.)

Over succeeding paragraphs, the paper goes through a point-by-point breakdown of its rationale for backing the Lib Dems, from criticism of the Conservatives to frustration at the incumbent Labour government's failure to embrace constitutional reform. Again, like all good leaders, it does so in the manner of an essay, culminating in this succinct summary of its policy reasons for switching sides:

> The Liberal Democrats were green before the other parties and remain so. Their commitment to education is bred in the bone. So is their comfort with a European project which, for all its flaws, remains central to this country's destiny. They are willing to contemplate a British defence policy without Trident renewal. They were right about Iraq, the biggest foreign policy judgement call of the past half-century, when Labour and the Tories were both catastrophically and stupidly wrong. They have resisted the rush to the overmighty centralised state when others have not.

(Ibid.)

Broadsheets do not have a monopoly on the art of framing a persuasive leader. Take this extract from the *Daily Mail* on the eve of the same election, in which it forcefully argues for a change of government, and criticizes Labour's record, from a very different political position to *The Guardian*'s. Beginning with a harsh assessment of then-Prime Minister Gordon Brown's economic legacy, it accuses him of being 'guilty of two grievous sins': a 'hubristic belief that he'd abolished boom-and-bust, which meant that he failed to put money aside during the boom years' and an 'almost religious belief in the power of the state to solve all life's problems'. Again, like a good essay, it goes on to itemize, one by one, a litany of policy failings it lays at Labour's door:

117

This has led him to squander untold billions of taxpayers' hard-earned money on expanding the public sector often to little discernible effect.

True, there have been improvements in healthcare – as you'd only expect, after the doubling of the NHS budget. Yet Britain remains at or near the bottom of the developed world's league tables for treating a range of conditions, from heart disease to cancer.

Even more damning, school standards are lower today than when Tony Blair came to power 13 years ago, chanting his mantra about education, education, education.

New Labour will also be remembered for corrupting the democratic process, politicising the Civil Service, turning judges into lawmakers through the Human Rights Act, emasculating the House of Lords and destroying a private pensions system that was once the envy of the world.

('Vote DECISIVELY to stop Britain walking blindly into disaster',
Daily Mail, 5 May 2010)

By contrast, the approach taken by the red-top *Sun* – Britain's biggest-selling daily newspaper and the one whose choice of party is traditionally seen as a barometer of the likely outcome – was decidedly less serious. Rather than focusing on more obviously important issues – health, education, social security or the economy – it instead chose to accuse both the Lib Dems and Labour of plotting a po-faced and joyless moral crusade to ban its iconic Page 3 slot, based on comments from two leading feminist politicians in the two camps who had indicated their desire to do so. In a tongue-in-cheek rant it described 'Page 3 girls in all their glory' as 'the very image of freedom' – a freedom now threatened, supposedly, by feminist killjoys.

In opting to make a semi-serious point about individual liberty versus 'big-state' interventionism in this way, *The Sun* was drawing on the tongue-in-cheek style its 'The Sun Says' leader column generally reserves for its second and/or third items.

Newspapers as 'Views-papers'

Op-ed articles are distinct from leaders, in that the views they give voice to are those of their by-lined authors. While these might well echo the worldview of the publication as a whole – it is not unreasonable to expect most *Daily Telegraph* comment writers to take a right-of-centre political perspective, for example, or those on *The Guardian* to do the opposite – this is not always the case. The latter paper, for instance, has adopted a more consciously inclusive op-ed policy in recent years, with, for example, right-leaning journalist Simon Jenkins becoming one of its regular contributors. Whatever political complexion op-ed pages cast on the title in which they appear, however, their choices of writers will tend to have one thing in common: in today's broadsheet newspapers and more highbrow and/or news-orientated magazines, they will generally be dominated by a relatively small, somewhat exclusive 'club' of prominent 'thinkers'. Though many of these will be journalists of one kind or other – from the *Daily Mail's* Melanie Phillips and Jan Moir to broadcaster Janet Street-Porter, who writes for the *Independent on Sunday* – others are authors (Clive Anderson, Howard Jacobson, Owen Jones) or politicians (Boris Johnson, Roy Hattersley), while still others might best be described as 'experts' in their fields. In almost all cases, whether someone is a regular or more occasional op-ed contributor, they will be presented as someone with a reasonable claim to 'authority' on the subject about which they are writing – however politically aligned, or one-sided, their perspective might be. And this authority, or expertise, must be on clear display in the comments they write if their arguments are to persuade us (the readers) that their ideas are valid and meaningful.

The following short extract comes from a February 2013 column in the Labour-supporting *New Statesman* weekly, written by the magazine's economics editor, David Blanchflower. As professor of economics at Dartmouth College, New Hampshire, and a former member of the Bank of England's monetary policy committee – the state-funded body which sets British interest rates – Blanchflower's 'qualifications' for this role are obvious. And, while his Keynesian take on the economy and left-leaning politics might be a turn-off for readers of other persuasions, at their best his columns offer textbook illustrations of how to frame convincing op-ed arguments using solid supporting evidence. In this particular column, Blanchflower returns to one of his pet subjects – the level of UK unemployment – and argues that figures produced by the Conservative-Liberal Democrat Coalition government to show that job cuts in the public sector have been more than cancelled out by rising employment in the private sector are misleading:

> The government's claim that it has created a million private-sector jobs is false. Over the past two years public-sector employment has fallen 521,000 while private-sector employment has increased by just over one million, a net increase of about half a million jobs. But of the one million 'new' private-sector jobs the coalition claims were 'created', a fifth were obtained by cheating, because lecturers in further education and sixth-form colleges were reclassified from the public to the private sector last spring. Fiddling the data isn't the same as creating private-sector jobs.
>
> (David Blanchflower, 'Decoding the unemployment figures exposes the truth behind the Coalition's spin', *New Statesman*, 28 February 2013)

A common attribute of many tabloid opinion columns is their deliberately provocative tone and use of language. For this reason, the more outspoken columnists – *The Sun's* Katie Hopkins or the *Daily Mail's* Richard Littlejohn – are sometimes likened to the (invariably right-wing) 'shock-jocks' that man the decks on many independent radio stations in the USA. The following extract from a Littlejohn column is typical of his particular style of articulate, highly partisan rant – railing, as it does, against the mass immigration he believes was presided over by Tony Blair and Gordon Brown's 'New Labour' govern-ments (one of his long-standing bugbears):

> Two former Labour Home Secretaries are being congratu-lated on their belated candour about immigration. Jack Straw

now says letting so many people settle in Britain was a 'spectacular mistake'.

David Blunkett has gone further, warning of civil unrest in his home city of Sheffield because the behaviour of recently arrived Roma gypsies is 'aggravating' the locals.

Joy there is said to be in Heaven over every repentant sinner. But before the angels start cracking open the Bollinger, it is worth pausing to consider the part played by both men in creating the mess we find ourselves in today. Straw and Blunkett were two of the most senior figures of the Blair/Brown era. They were fully signed up to the New Labour 'project'.

> (Littlejohn, 'Immigration a mistake? Come off it, Jack Straw!',
> *Daily Mail*, 14 November 2013)

While Littlejohn's idiosyncratic style may be a world away from the more sober writing of left-wing commentators like *The Guardian's* Polly Toynbee or George Monbiot – or, for that matter, their Conservative-leaning stable-mate, Jenkins – the former is no less adept at packing his columns with (carefully chosen) facts and figures to 'justify' his frequently controversial views. In the column quoted previously, for example, Littlejohn goes on to stake out his contentious conspiracy theory about Labour's secret motives for supposedly opening the flood-gates to foreign immigrants with persuasive rhetorical flourishes that steer close to polemic. Narrowly avoiding libelling former Labour ministers, he writes:

> Labour set out utterly to transform the demographic make-up of England without making any attempt to obtain democratic consent.
>
> I say 'England' specifically, because it is England which has borne the brunt of mass immigration and is now struggling to live with the consequences.
>
> New Labour hated the English. We weren't to be trusted. In 2000, Straw himself damned the English as violent nationalists who have used force to subjugate other races. It was a despicable slur, but entirely in keeping with Labour's

121

core strategy.

That preposterous Welsh-born oaf Two Jags [former Deputy Prime Minister John Prescott], who demeaned high office for a decade, even claimed: 'There is no such nationality as English.'

The fear was that the love affair with New Labour wouldn't last and the English would revert to type and return a Conservative government. So the plan was to flood the country with immigrants who would then repay the favour by voting Labour.

(Ibid.)

Comment-based Blogs

In the next chapter, we will switch our focus to examining the various new forms of digital-era journalistic writing in detail – from content-writing for the websites of government departments and multinational corporations to the use of social media by eyewitness citizen journalists to live blogging and tweeting by mainstream news reporters from the scenes of unfolding stories. However, no discussion of the more subjective forms of journalism explored in this chapter would be complete without at least acknowledging the contribution to the field of comment-based blogs.

When more journalistic (as opposed to personal) web-logs (or blogs) first began to proliferate online in the early noughties, they were overwhelmingly oriented towards comment, rather than breaking news. Taking their lead from America (as ever, ahead of most countries in embracing new online trends), more opinionated British bloggers sank their teeth into the worlds of politics and, to a lesser extent, the arts with barely concealed relish. While many of the more prominent political and cultural bloggers have since turned their hands to other, more sophisticated, forms of online and multimedia journalism – examples of which we examine in the next chapter – a decade ago their sites were decidedly more lo-fi and linear in nature. While the best of them were ably written in an engagingly informal, even conversational, style, most were decidedly patchy affairs, in terms of the quality of their prose, and their appeal arose almost entirely from their content – usually a mix of *Punch-* or *Private Eye*-inspired satirical humour, gossip column/ diary page-style tittle-tattle and no-holds-barred rants. Over time, however, the more popular (for which read 'most-visited') sites began to become more plugged in to the political and cultural establishment – with the result that, today, like the best political and arts journalists, they increasingly find themselves receiving highly newsworthy 'tip-offs' from in-the-know contacts and 'breaking' stories with the momentum to influence, if not lead, the mainstream news agenda. The following extract is from one of a succession of much-publicized posts on the UK's best-known political blog site, www.orderorder.org, brainchild of right-wing commentator Guido Fawkes (aka Paul Staines). In it, 'Guido' – as ever, referring to himself in the third person – rages against Downing Street special advisor Damian McBride for allegedly feeding a series of smears against prominent Tory politicians to a Labour-supporting scandal site, www.theredrag. co.uk. These claims, first exposed by the blogger, were to become the subject of a feverish national media debate in ensuing days – ultimately leading to McBride's dismissal:

> Downing Street under Gordon Brown has been particularly vicious in smearing opponents. Other well-known Labour insiders besides Damian McBride – including a government minister – are involved in the operation. Guido has hard evidence that Tory MPs have been smeared, and that a particularly vicious concerted smear operation was mounted against George Osborne, smears that Damian McBride – a civil servant – knows and admits in writing are untrue, yet he was still instrumental in spreading. Some well-known lobby journalists have knowingly gone along with it. This is a lot bigger than some minor bloggers spat.
>
> (Guido Fawkes, 'McBride spinning for his career',
> www.Order-Order.com, 11 April 2009)

More recently, blogging has become a favoured tool of campaign groups, charities and non-government organizations (NGOs) with particular political, social and/or economic objectives. Indeed, a number of these – for example, Amnesty International, Friends of the Earth and Shelter – have harnessed it in an avowedly journalistic way, generating not only comment pieces but also features and stories (often written by supporters with reporting backgrounds) in an effort to highlight particular causes or injustices. Their efforts – bringing to light issues that, in earlier times, one might have expected to be uncovered by bona fide investigative journalists – are a latter-day manifestation of the 'crusading' journalism once diligently undertaken by the press, as explored in Chapter 4. It is apt that we should end this chapter with an example of such campaigning prose from one of Britain's foremost blog-writers, Justin McKeating, a trained news journalist and author of *The Blog Digest*, who now works as environmental charity Greenpeace's official blogger on the nuclear industry:

> Well, now we know; the reason for widespread public distrust of nuclear power is because way back in 1962, Dr No – the evil scientist in the James Bond film of the same name – built a nuclear reactor on a Jamaican island and used it to threaten the world.
>
> At least that's the reason given for the shadow cast over the image of nuclear power by Professor David Phillips, of the UK's prestigious Royal Society of Chemistry. Fortunately for us all, British secret agent James Bond thwarted Dr No. But unfortunately for the nukes industry, the public has had a 'remorselessly grim' (Professor Phillips' words) view of nuclear power ever since it was exposed to Dr No's nefarious plan.
>
> There's no doubt Professor Phillips is an eminent and respected scientist. Awarded the Order of the British Empire (OBE) by the Queen in 1999 for services to science education and made a Commander of the Order of the British Empire (CBE) in January 2012 for services to chemistry, he is an author, broadcaster and a leader in his field.
>
> However, his blaming the fact that nuclear power is

distrusted, feared and otherwise shunned by many people, on a 50-year-old spy movie has to be one of the worst pieces of pro-nuclear propaganda we've ever seen (and we thought we'd seen them all).

(Iain McKeating, 'British scientist blames James Bond villain for unpopularity of nuclear power', www.greenpeace.org, 12 January 2012)

Here, in one neat package, we have an example of the blog at its most effective: a sharp, witty, well-structured piece of campaigning polemic combining a serious message with the kind of news sense and flair for a dropped intro that can only come with experience of other forms of journalistic writing. The next chapter will pick up where this one leaves off, by taking a more wide-ranging look at the rapid evolution of journalistic writing in the digital age – from hyper-local news reporting to collaborative social media and investigative sites to discursive micro-blogs like Twitter and Tumblr.

7. JOURNALISM ON THE GO: FROM LIVE TWEETING TO ONLINE CONTENT-WRITING

ONLINE JOURNALISTIC WRITING HAS evolved to such an extent over the past decade or more that it is no longer sufficient (or, strictly speaking, accurate) to speak of it as *online* journalism at all. Today, journalistic 'content' – a word, to which we will return, that has become a bugbear of many traditional practitioners – is consumed, and increasingly produced, on such a wide range of platforms, for so many divergent niche and mainstream audiences that, if it can be bracketed at all under a single heading, that heading would be *digital*. Today one can barely walk down the high street, let alone catch a bus or a train, without encountering hordes of people with their heads down, eyes trained not on printed pages but the screens of myriad digital 'devices'. And while many will be emailing friends, playing games, streaming films or TV programmes, or even reading books they have downloaded from the Internet, ever-more people are accessing their news, and perusing their lifestyle magazines, using web-based subscriptions and applications, rather than conventional print media.

As this does not presume to be a technical book (except, in the loosest sense, with regard to the written word), this chapter will not even attempt to explain the technology behind apps, tablet computers, mobile smartphones or the like. What it has to address, however, is some of the ways in which the proliferation of these new devices, and the content management and operating systems they have spawned, has contributed to a rapid evolution in the nature and form(s) of journalistic writing itself. Chapters 1 and 2 have already touched on the ways in which traditional publications have responded to the need to generate copy for their online, as well as print, editions, and some of the considerations they have taken into account as they have adapted their article formats, and lengths, to suit the web page. For this reason, we will not re-tread this ground here, but rather widen our horizons to examine the more radical, even platform-specific, ways in which journalistic writing – and the practice of journalism itself – has been transformed to suit the needs and demands of today's on-the-go, interactive multimedia audiences. Our journey will take us way beyond those early experiments in citizen journalism briefly explored at the end of Chapter 6 to look in more detail at how many of the bold pioneers of yesterday's blogsphere have helped shape practices that are today considered essential components of the day-to-day toolkit of journalists working in the mainstream media.

So fluid – and so rapidly evolving – has written journalism become in the digital sphere that it is impossible to give anything approaching a comprehensive overview of these manifestations in a book of this kind. However, it is always possible to identify patterns and spot trends that can lay claim to some prospect of longevity, and it is to this task, principally, that we turn in this chapter. As with every subject, however, there are some things that refuse to be pigeonholed, and to this end we will close the chapter – and the first part of the book – with a brief examination of a form of journalistic writing that transcends distinctions between print and online/digital. This is the nebulous arena known as 'copy/content-writing' that embraces contributions to (among other things) brochures, government and corporate PR/marketing campaigns and, especially, websites – the demands on which have grown exponentially in this globally interconnected, and ever-more consumer-orientated age.

The onset of the digital era has led to three key transformations in the styles and modes of everyday journalistic writing: greater speed, tighter brevity, and the increasingly routine involvement of audience-members themselves in the reporting and publishing process. Of these, perhaps the most revolutionary change has been the democratization of journalistic output. Much has been made of this so-called 'citizen journalism' and its associated benefits (and hazards) – particularly its contribution to our knowledge about issues and events in 'closed' and/or seldom-reported societies and the empowerment it potentially bestows on ordinary members of the public everywhere, by freeing them from a dependency on traditional 'top-down' flows of information from trained professionals with privileged access to 'in-the-know' sources. In the context of this book, however, it is noteworthy primarily for its effects on journalistic *writing*. And perhaps the most significant of these has been its steady erosion of the 'standardization' that previously distinguished different types of journalistic article – marking out the news story from the feature from the review from the comment piece. While these categories (and the stylistic attributes that characterize them) remain remarkably resilient in the realm of print journalism, not so online, where the new medium has in some ways 'dictated' that new forms be adopted, while at the same time 'freeing' writers from constraints imposed by the old. To take one simple illustration, while print newspapers and magazines are finite publications, with a set number of pages each issue that need to be written, designed, sent off to the printers and distributed to retailers, their (various) digital versions occupy a potentially limitless space, with scope to publish far more articles, or individual pieces of much greater length and complexity. To this extent, online boasts a clear advantage over print – its only limitations being the number of journalists (amateur and professional) it can afford to pay, or otherwise persuade, to write for it.

As for speed, while this has always been of the essence in journalism, particularly in news-reporting, today's journalists are expected to be able to upload online their 'first takes' on a story within minutes of piecing together the bare bones of what has happened (or is happening), updating and otherwise adding to them in piecemeal 'chunks' of copy as and when they have more detail to disclose. Increasingly, they are also expected to write their own headlines and captions – removing from the equation the filter of the dedicated sub-editor, whose sharpening up of their raw journalistic prose was once viewed as a crucial stage in the 'writing' process. Today everyone is his or her own sub (up to a point), and it is often left to informed audience-members to pick up on errors and omissions in a journalist's copy, at the point that they tweet their feedback or post a comment on an online discussion-thread. From a writing point of view, though, the enhanced speed afforded by digital publishing has led to several other significant transformations in the way journalism now appears online – with many unfolding stories, from general elections to government budget statements to Champions League match reports, being told in a form that fuses 'objective' reporting with (subjective) blow-by-blow commentary, often flowing (in a somewhat awkward marriage) from the 'pen' of the same journalist. And, just as citizen journalists have appraised us of stories from remote or otherwise inaccessible trouble-spots we might never previously have heard about, so, too, do members of the public now regularly contribute to the more mundane day-to-day exchanges of information (and views) that accompany 'routine' breaking news. The result is that, when published, these highly collaborative 'live feeds' and 'live blogs' appear to those reading them in the form of a scrolling montage of reported details and emailed/tweeted opinions, with different posters often directly taking issue with each other's views and/or versions of events. How many worlds away this is from the 'authoritative', single-author journalistic writing that until recently typified the way reporting was presented to the public.

So we are left with brevity as the last of our three great, transformative trends in journalistic writing – a curiosity, in some ways, given the aforementioned point about the 'infinity' of space that is available for publications to exploit on the Internet. In the context of digital, brevity can perhaps best be understood as a function of the speed described above. If reporters have less time to get their stories 'up and running', and only need to have found out enough for their opening paragraphs by the time they are expected to have posted their first dispatches, by definition much of what they write is liable to be short and to-the-point. Moreover, implicit in the new rule of thumb about the 'need for speed' is a commercially driven recognition by journalistic outlets that the instantaneous nature of modern communications – combined with the ever-more hectic lives most of us lead – means that people want to receive their information more quickly and succinctly than ever. The fact that news can travel so fast these days, then, means it now invariably *has* to. The fact that people in developed societies are working more hours, and travelling longer distances between home and work, creates a demand for 'journalism on the go' – and news and views that can be 'consumed' in flexible formats customized to the multifarious devices, from smartphones to mp3 players to tablet computers, on which we are accessing them. The more rapidly available, handily packaged and 'visual' these updates the better, whether this involves conveying them in neat little sentences, tightly edited video clips and/or pithy, bite-sized 'articles'. This, at least, has been the received wisdom guiding the practices of most editors and publishers during the first decade or more of online journalism, and it is to the main developments in journalistic writing this has spawned that we now turn.

Live Blogging and Tweeting

So influential has been the rise of online social media, and the citizen journalism at the forefront of harnessing it, that it is perhaps apt to begin by evaluating the characteristics of the single trend in journalistic writing that has done most to blend all three of our transforming factors: speed, brevity and audience participation. In live blogging – and, latterly, tweeting – we have the clearest example of how technological tools initially embraced principally by 'amateurs' have the power to revolutionize the day-to-day practices of 'professionals'. For one thing, any dividing-line between these two 'factions' is fast dissolving: the conventional gatekeeper role of the cinema or music critic, for example, is harder than ever to sustain in an age when anyone with a reliable broadband Internet connection can stream movie clips and preview tracks ahead of the official release of the film or album from which they are taken, allowing them to write their own reviews and, more importantly, make their own minds up about the work without having to rely on the recommendations of professional critics with privileged access. More to the point, in many cases it has been citizens, not 'journalists', who have led the way in recognizing the potential of digital communications. A stark illustration of the dynamic and interactive 'two-way' – or 'multi-directional' – exchanges between news professionals, 'expert' commentators and 'amateur' contributors (you and me) that is becoming commonplace in the live online coverage published each spring by the likes of www.bbc.co.uk and www.guardian.co.uk as Britain's Chancellor of the Exchequer announces his Budget. From start to finish, these websites' rolling budget threads can run for as long as twelve hours – from 6 a.m., when the day's speculation about the contents of the Government's major annual economic statement begins in earnest with the opening credits of BBC Radio 4's *Today* programme, to a final post sometime after 5 p.m., focusing on a particular headline announcement or announcements that sum up the overall spirit, and underlying agenda, of the speech. What follows is a fictionalized extract from a 'typical' BBC or broadsheet newspaper live Budget thread – with emails from audience-members liberally interspersed with staff reporters' hurried summaries of key points in the speech (and responses to it) and opinionated tweets from assorted pundits, academics, lobby groups and 'expert' journalists from both within and without the organization:

16:39: Mr Michaels [the Chancellor] warned that a slight drop in forecast tax receipts from the banking sector shows how important it is for the Government not to be deviated from its 'long-term economic plan' in pursuit of short-term tax cuts or giveaways. However, the British Banking Association says in reply: 'We anticipate that the fiscal contribution from the banking sector for 2014–15 will be in line with the Treasury's stated expectations at the start of the tax year.'

16:50: Shadow Chancellor Jon Summers tweets: 'Michaels' over-optimistic figures at start of yr show how much we need annual bankers' bonus tax.'

Via Twitter Iain Stuart, ITV News Business, tweets: CBI warns that pensions changes 'cd pose unsustainable burden for employers, esp SMEs.'

16:55: Director general of the Association of British Pension Funds Saskia Ramonescu says the changes to pensions 'amount to an unprecedented challenge' for her sector that may well result in 'many more people being forced to rely on state top-up' and/or the personalized private pensions sector'.

16:57: ... Susie Bryant, Godalming, emails: 'The increase in the tax breaks for the middle classes is great for those with professional jobs and an ability to save but for me on a pension of £9,687 and my daughter on the minimum wage at £8,890 we will never be able to save.'

As the example illustrates, live blogs can take some decoding for the uninitiated. To those who grew up in the analogue era, rolling online feeds bear little or no resemblance to traditional newspaper reports and/or TV and radio bulletins, in which journalists ('they') would tell the audience ('us') what was going on in the world, and indicate what it all *meant* – based on some element of 'delay' between an event occurring and its being reported, which allowed them to filter and interpret (however roughly) the most salient information. Although such forms of top-down journalistic expression have survived, to some extent, in print (as witnessed in the earlier chapters), many newspapers, magazines and broadcast media organizations now adopt very different approaches to the coverage they publish online, as seen here. And the blizzard of hash-tagged comments mined by web editors from micro-blogging site Twitter, Facebook and emails/ text messages sent direct to their news organizations by those following their coverage have brought with them various other new traits that one would never have encountered in old-style journalistic writing. Chief among these is a highly abbreviated form of writing sentences – with tweeted sound-bites limited to 140 characters and even individual words and phrases reduced to vowel-less 'outlines' of their correct compositions. The fictional ITV journalist's tweet, quoted above, is a case in point: in order to force it to conform to the required character limit, he has abbreviated the word 'could' to 'cld' and 'especially' to 'esp', apparently confident that readers familiar with SMS 'text-speak' will have little or no trouble deciphering his meaning.

While it is possible to identify and recognize the stylistic tropes that typify this new form of 24/7, digitally driven news reporting, however, to what extent do they offer us forms of writing worthy of serious critical appreciation? Comparing what (for the most part) amount to single-line factual updates, or opinions that (however well articulated) 'shoot straight from the hip' almost as soon as something has been reported with the more considered (if at times indulgent) news reports and comment pieces fashioned by seasoned print professionals is clearly as meaningless as lining up the proverbial apples and oranges. Rather, what tweets, text messages and Facebook posts have to contribute to the onward progression of journalistic expression arguably lies in the effectiveness with which they manage to harness the one quality they hold in common: their enforced brevity. When tweeted updates or reaction quotes really hit their mark is on the occasions they bring clarity to a subject or deliver an opinion with razor-sharp precision – distilling the essence of something worth reporting or 'saying' to a few well-chosen words. Just as the great stylists of old, from Hemingway to Orwell, had much to teach us about the value of using plain language and economical sentences to describe world-changing events or social experiences, the most skilled and adept of today's 'Twitterati' are busily defining what it means to speak of journalistic concision today. *Channel 4 News* anchor Jon Snow, BBC presenter Samira Ahmed and columnist Owen Jones are among today's most prolific journalist-tweeters.

Multi-dimensional Multimedia Story-telling

If live blogging and tweeting represent the (still-fledgling) digital medium's biggest single contribution to date to the refinement of 'reporterly' writing, there is one other key way in which the advent of online has transformed the nature of routine journalistic writing. This is the form of reporting/feature-writing popularly known as 'three-dimensional' – or 'multidimensional' – story-telling. In the early days of the Internet, web-based articles tended to be written (or reproduced) for online in much the same 'linear' format they would be in print: that is to say, what readers were presented with was a straightforward piece of writing which, as far as possible, replicated the inverted pyramid or diamond structures of, respectively, a typical news story or feature. This was particularly true of articles published online by already established print newspapers and magazines, which tended to simply transplant their 'hard copy' – with accompanying pictures and headlines intact – onto their websites. The new medium, then, was being forced (not always successfully) to adapt to the content, rather than the other way round. By contrast, what has happened since the advent of so-called 'web 2.0' – the point, during the mid-2000s, when consumers began to access the Internet on their mobile phones, as well as computers, and communicate and share information via social networking services like Facebook and Twitter – is that *articles* (*content*) have increasingly been adapted for the *medium*.

In recent times, this customization of newspaper and magazine content has reached a new level, with bespoke applications (apps) developed to deliver versions of what are essentially the same articles to individual digital platforms and branded devices – from Apple iPads to Android smartphones and tablets. But, speaking more generally, the enduring contribution of web 2.0 to the development of journalistic writing has been its fostering of a more visual, far less linear, approach to telling stories and informing the public. Where three-dimensional story-telling differs from the simple 'cut and paste' approach to publishing online of old is that it explicitly harnesses the unique multimedia attributes of the Internet to find new, more lateral and interactive, ways of presenting journalism. One way of conceiving of this approach is to see these new, three-dimensional, articles not as stories or features with a simple trajectory – leading the reader from A to B to C – but rather as multi-directional 'maps', which can navigate them along any of a number of related routes that, once explored in full, will offer a much more rounded, in-depth understanding of a subject than the necessarily selective stories and features of the past. The best illustration of how this approach works in practice is the revolutionary introduction of the hyperlink: a link to another web page, or website, which can be embedded within an online article to guide readers to additional background on a key term, individual, institution or event referred to in the text. Hyperlinks – denoted by their trademark underlining, often in a different colour to the rest of the text – are now so much a part of the furniture of online articles, wherever they are published, that most of us scarcely notice them when we come across them. However, at the time they first began to appear, it is hard to describe how much of a paradigm shift they presented to online readers, as they found themselves able to break off from reading an article to quickly bone up on the history of this event or the biography of that celebrity or politician at the click of a mouse.

Three-dimensionality has not only come about through hyperlinks, though. Another facet of online publishing which marks it out from print is its ability to add lustre to written articles, where appropriate, with the addition of sound and moving images. Again, we see this form of enhanced story-telling routinely today. A story on the *Guardian*, *Telegraph* or BBC websites about a political dispute between rival parties is likely to incorporate video and/or audio clips of the opposing players making their case – sometimes recorded especially to accompany the article, on other occasions lifted from the radio or TV programmes on which the comments or statements prompting the story were originally made. Other innovations that have further added to the multi-dimensionality of online journalism include the incorporation of user-generated content (UGC) – from photos and videos snatched by eyewitnesses to unfolding news events on their mobile phones to written testimony posted on websites' collaborative blogs, discussion-threads, Twitter, Facebook and other social media platforms.

Although most mainstream media outlets have now embraced the new multi-dimensional approach to story-telling (however reluctantly, in some cases), its most enthusiastic and sophisticated proponents include political bloggers and other forms of citizen journalist. One such pioneer is Sunny Hundal, the founder of www.liberalconspiracy.org – which was, until its closure in 2014, Britain's leading left-leaning political blog site. Though much of the site's content was (like many blogs) reactive and comment-based, it published many articles that more closely resembled stories and features, often devoting considerable space to exploring complex subjects in more depth than a simple news report would allow. The following extract – with hyperlinks underlined as they were on the site – gives a flavour of the multi-dimensional approach it adopted to directing readers to examine issues it reported on in more depth:

In January this year around 40 Sikhs <u>attacked and vandalised</u> a restaurant in Leicester, alleging that a young Sikh girl had been raped in a room above the restaurant. The police <u>denied rumours</u> and the allegations, and some of the attackers were prosecuted. But it later emerged that a group of men *had* used that room to <u>exploit a vulnerable teenager for sex</u>, repeatedly.

The Leicester case was a key part of a <u>BBC1 report last Monday</u> that British Sikh girls were being groomed for sex by gangs of men, primarily of Muslim background. The programme was horrifying and saddening to watch. Some of the girls, just barely teenagers, had been tricked by men pretending to be Sikh and then groomed until they were raped. In some cases they were drugged, photographed naked and then blackmailed into rape and abuse. It has caused a furore amongst British Sikhs and a worryingly large number say on public forums that they're willing to take the law into their own hands to protect Sikh women, as the police are seen as ineffectual.

Nothing strains Hindu-Sikh-Muslim relations like seeing women of their religion being preyed on by men of other religions. Tensions between British Sikhs and Muslims are now at a new low, having come close to boiling point in several instances, <u>most notably in Luton in late May</u>. [Rumours quickly spread via forums like this: 'Sikh Girl Dragged Into Wooded Area And Raped By Paki' – which was never confirmed.]

(Sunny Hundal, 'Sikhs v Muslims: why the debate on grooming isn't about the women themselves', www.liberalconspiracy.org, *12 September 2013*)

Where standard press reports would have customarily reported this issue in a (quite literally) 'straight down the line' way, using an inverted pyramid news structure or diamond-style feature format to relay only the 'hard facts' about the alleged crimes or, at best, briefly explore conflicting accounts in a marginally more in-depth manner, here Hundal weaves into his narrative – itself a much freer mix of reporting and commentary than one tends to encounter in traditional print articles – a blizzard of steers and signposts. These steers and signposts largely take the form of numerous hyperlinks – some pointing readers towards the original reports on which his own article focuses; others referring them to the sources of the claims and counter-claims on which those reports were based, so they are in a better position to make up their own minds about the veracity of the alleged offences. Taken together, what the article as a whole and the various secondary sources to which it directs readers achieve is a much more holistic and meaningful representation of a highly sensitive and contentious issue than one would expect to find in the more formulaic structures familiar from print.

Crowd-sourced and Collaborative Investigative Reporting

The final distinct trend in journalistic writing to have emerged with the advent of web 2.0 owes a debt to certain aspects of the multi-dimensional story-telling model, but nonetheless boasts several attributes that are unique to it, on account of its particular *raison d'être*. This is the collaborative investigative feature: an increasingly popular variety of online article, in which a journalist attempts to get beneath the skin of a complex topic or debate by explicitly inviting readers to work with him or her to uncover the full facts behind it or offer fresh perspectives on it. Often, readers will be given a certain degree of freedom to contribute anything they feel is relevant – from eyewitness testimony to vicarious experience to 'expert' knowledge based on their professional training or background. Sometimes, they will be given much more specific missions: for example, to press their local councils or MPs for particular information or even to help the journalist plough through a large body of data or lengthy document they have published online, in search of newsworthy patterns/angles. In recent times, *The Guardian* and the *Daily Telegraph* have been the UK papers to embrace such practices most keenly, with the former recruiting its readers to identify stories buried in the mountain of detail 'info-dumped' by parliamentary authorities in relation to MPs' expenses claims in 2008–9, and the latter running an ongoing sub-site devoted to finding evidence of profligate spending by local authorities from the sea of data routinely published under transparency rules introduced in 2010.

This collaborative approach to news-gathering has come to be known as *crowd-sourcing*. And, as ever, from the point of view of this book, it is primarily of interest in relation to the impact it has had on the process and presentation of journalistic *writing*. The following extract is typical of the way such an article commonly appears on screen. The journalist will tend to introduce it with a scene-setting preamble, followed by several paragraphs in which he or she outlines the method used to investigate an issue and their provisional findings. Journalists will then invite readers to follow their example and notify them (and *fellow* readers) when they have something else interesting to report. These nuggets of additional, user-generated information will then be woven into the fabric of the article as and when they are submitted – or, to be more precise, once they have been verified by the journalist 'anchoring' the article, in a process known as 'moderation'. The finished article (to the extent it is ever totally finished, given the ability of readers to continue contributing to it, at least in theory, for some time after it first starts 'running') will come to resemble something akin to a tapestry – its individual strands slowly weaving together to create an ever-more complete picture of a (typically) tangled and contested issue. In the extract, *Guardian* journalist Polly Curtis anchors a collaborative investigation into the grassroots impact of a then-controversial government policy to 'cap' the levels of housing benefit that could be claimed by those in receipt of social security payments living in different sizes of properties. The policy's critics had claimed it would lead to 'social cleansing' from inner-city areas in London and the south-east, as claimants would be priced out of districts in which their benefits would no longer cover the cost of their housing – forcing them to relocate to outer suburbs and cheaper locations elsewhere. The object of the investigation was twofold: to find out if this was actually happening in general terms and, more specifically, whether households receiving housing benefit that had been forced to move on grounds of cost were able to find private-sector landlords and agencies willing to house them. In common with many such articles, it opens by staking out its 'peg', in these straightforward terms:

> From this year a new cap on housing benefit has limited weekly payments to: £250 a week for a one bedroom property (including shared accommodation); £290 a week for a two bedroom property; £340 a week for a three bedroom property; and £400 a week for a four bedroom property. At the moment only people who are moving house are affected but within a year the cap will be in place across the country. Today there are reports that the London Borough of Newham has approached Stoke-on-Trent asking them to consider taking 500 families who have been priced out of the area.
>
> (Polly Curtis, 'Will the housing benefit cap cause the 'social cleansing' of London?', www.guardian.co.uk, 24 April 2012)

It is a third of the way down the article, though, that it starts to truly display the distinctive characteristics of the collaborative online investigation, with a scene-setter that dispenses with the customary 'rules' barring the use of the first person from reporting, in a section headed 'analysis':

I've looked at the housing minister's initial claim that there are more than 1,000 private rental properties currently available in Newham and within a five mile radius. I've repeated his search without a price limit and without a bedroom requirement and there are indeed thousands available.

I searched for a four bedroom property within five miles of Newham and with a cap of £400 and there are 339 properties available. The cheapest, a very nice looking four bedroom house in E11 is advertised at the very unlikely price of £81 a week (which looks like a mistake).

(Ibid.)

In this case, the punchline comes when Curtis shows her hand with a series of findings that cast grave doubt on the government's claims that cheap properties are available to claimants:

I called the agents and asked whether this was available to housing benefit tenants and was told 'definitely not'. I called a random selection and of the four or five estate agents that answered the phone (it was before 9 am) none said that the property within the band could be paid through housing benefits.

(Ibid.)

And, a little beneath this, we encounter the first fruits of Curtis's call to arms to aid her investigation, in the form of a string of tweeted exchanges between her and various readers who have got in contact to correct, and in some cases enhance, information she has reported earlier:

10.03am: Need to correct one point in my Rightmove research. @nigenet tweets:
@pollycurtis That 4 bed for £81/week http://t.co/hSNPoFTR is actually 1 room in a shared house. Still not a bad price though.
Apologies for that, the property was mis-listed.

(Ibid.)

What these extracts illustrate, in sum, is the increasingly fluid nature of online journalistic writing in general, and online reporting in particular. In many ways, there is nothing structured or complete about this latter example at all: instead, it follows a much less prescriptive path than most traditional journalism, growing organically as and when new information comes to light, and new contributions are made by the potentially limitless army of writers it has mobilized to add to its narrative. In terms of journalistic writing, what comes out 'on the page' is peculiarly unformed: there is no cohesive prose 'style' to speak of, principally because of the multiplicity of 'voices' contributing to the whole. As a piece of raw, unvarnished journalism, though, it is arguably none the worse for this.

A Few Words about Content-writing

Though content-writing – or copy-writing, to use its other name – is by no means a new phenomenon, it has undoubtedly gained a fresh lease of life in the digital era. Few journalists enter the profession with a burning desire to write customized copy for government departments, local authorities, corporations or charities, but for those struggling to make a living out of freelancing it can provide a crucial fall-back during months when commissions for 'proper' journalistic articles are thin on the ground. In the online era, every organization of any size needs its own website – and, far from being mere 'shop windows' for organizations to ply their wares, today's 'online presences' tend to be increasingly interactive, situated entities in their own right, with their own brand identities, sales teams, social media platforms, information hubs and all manner of other 'whistles and bells' tailored to the heavily market-researched (or presumed) needs and wishes of their intended 'audience'.

'Content', then, has evolved rapidly in the online era – in some ways, even more so than journalism itself. Whereas just ten years ago it would have been fine for a company or council to have little more than a homepage, containing a brief statement of purpose and, perhaps, a few links to contact pages and one or two directly relevant external sites, today's corporate, government and charity websites need to be bubbling, fizzing, 24/7 affairs, replete with (now almost obligatory) Twitter feeds, Facebook pages, discussion-threads and/or customer forums. Keeping the latter bubbling alone – and 'moderating' them to ensure content posted by participating visitors, or 'users', remains within the bounds of the law – is itself an increasingly full-time job. In this instance, who better to employ to carry out these roles than experienced journalists: professional writers who themselves have had to adapt rapidly to the demands of this new, two-way era of news-making and communication in their day-to-day journalistic writing?

Aside from the social media aspects of content-writing/online interaction, though, where else do journalistic writing skills come in useful in the process of generating this content? One key source of work (and income) for jobbing freelance journalists – not to mention some of those who move, wholesale, into any number of related industries, from public relations to marketing – is the production of press releases, mission statements, background papers, and even, increasingly, bespoke 'features' purporting to be objective pieces of journalism to bring to life and 'big up' the achievements and objectives of the organization for whom they are written, through the liberal (and selective) use of statistics, interviews, human-interest case studies and all manner of other journalistic devices.

This is not (heaven forbid) a book about how to write PR, let alone the literature of marketing or corporate communications. However, it would not be complete without a very brief overview of this increasingly ubiquitous (and, for journalists, lucrative) area of what might (very broadly) be termed journalistic writing. In the digital age, it is perhaps most instructive to divide content-writing into two broad categories, each of which we will briefly examine: general website copy-writing/editing and 'short-form' news feeds, flashes, and updates for digital and mobile platforms.

A guideline to bear in mind in *all* types of commercial copy-writing (which is essentially what producing 'content' amounts to) is that it is at its most persuasive – and, therefore, effective

– when it succeeds in 'selling' something to its readers without *appearing* to. In other words, the copy-writer who manages to catch and hold the attention of prospective customers without 'trying too hard' – by over-ingratiating him/herself or lavishing the copy with too obvious or clichéd a sales pitch – is doing the job well, and in all likelihood will have pleased whoever commissioned him/her. Plain, simple but punchy prose is called for: writing that explains, un-fussily, what a product, service and/or organization has to offer, without getting too bogged down in detail or, conversely, over-simplifying something that is genuinely complex. In many respects, then, a similar rule applies to that emphasized in Chapter 1's exploration of the art of news-writing: less is often more in good copy/content-writing.

The following example is taken from one of the main home-pages (there are several) on the official website of the European Union, http://europa.eu. Though it is reasonable to assume that many of those visiting this site to brush up on the origins and purpose of the EU will be sufficiently educated and/or informed to make sense of it, this content is flawed in a number of ways – not least its use of meaningless vagaries ('towards its full potential') and repetition (the term 'economic cooperation' appears twice in the second paragraph). The overriding impression is one of the writer falling into the trap of uncritically regurgitating received (and highly bureaucratic) jargon, rather than adequately translating it into language likely to 'mean' something to the layperson:

> The EU is a unique economic and political partnership between 28 European countries that together cover much of the continent.
>
> The EU was created in the aftermath of the Second World War. The first steps were to foster economic cooperation: the idea being that countries who trade with one another become economically interdependent and so more likely to avoid conflict. The result was the European Economic Community (EEC), created in 1958, and initially increasing economic cooperation between six countries: Belgium, Germany, France, Italy, Luxembourg and the Netherlands. Since then,

a huge single market has been created and continues to develop towards its full potential.

If the writer of this copy is a trained journalist, this makes it all the more infuriating, as its style appears to have been forcibly tailored to conform to the rigid demands of an officious bureaucracy. If, however, the copy is this dry and lifeless because it has been penned by a team of civil servants or a committee of policy advisors, then it arguably should not have been – particularly if one of its aims is to reach, and engage, those with little or no prior knowledge of the EU's aims and objectives (as one can only assume it is).

Bureaucratic organizations like the EU do not, though, have a monopoly on vague and imprecise copy-writing. Take this example, which is loosely modelled on the 'what we do' section of the website of one of Britain's leading public relations agencies. Although the business of PR is about communicating 'messages' to the public via the media, the following mission statement could arguably do with substantial fine-tuning to improve its clarity:

> We represent our clients by crafting dynamic narratives that promote their brand, campaigns and causes. We use persuasive words, images and footage to provoke and pilot conversations. Our breadth of knowledge and influence ensures that these dialogues impact our clients' desired audiences and communities.
>
> Impacting in this way generates positive reputational benefits for our clients – in turn influencing and shaping the way key audiences and stakeholders behave towards their brands, campaigns and causes.

True, there is a certain amount of 'active' writing in here – in the shape of 'doing words' like 'creating, curating and editing' – but, for those not already versed in the jargon of the PR and marketing worlds, how clear a mental picture does this mission statement really project about the exact nature of the work in which the agency is engaged? The prose is steeped in 'media-speak', with its boast to be able to 'provoke and pilot conversations' (with *whom?* one might ask). And talk of influencing how 'key audiences and stakeholders behave towards their brands, campaigns and causes' is the sort of language that is only likely to make sense to those already familiar with the culture of PR (though, admittedly, it is for this audience, perhaps, that the statement is intended).

By way of contrast, consider the following handily 'hyperlinked' mission statement on the overall homepage of the British government's award-winning one-stop website, www.gov.uk:

> The websites of all <u>government departments</u> and many other agencies and public bodies are being merged into GOV.UK.
>
> Here you can see all <u>policies, announcements, publications, statistics,</u> and <u>consultations</u>.

Lean, mean and self-explanatory, this is a model of how online content-writing should appear. And this point returns us to one of the premises of this chapter. Today's audiences (like journalists) are people perpetually on the go – racing from one job, engagement, even leisure activity to another, and seldom sitting still for any length of time. Even if they are prepared to wade through what today would be considered a relatively long-form piece of writing – a feature, an essay or even a novel – they expect (and, to some extent, need) it to be expressed in a clear, concise form, with ambiguities, vagaries and obscure language kept to a minimum. The problem with the extract from the European Union and the fictional PR websites quoted previously is not so much that they are too long-winded or detailed – in many ways, neither gives us enough information about precisely what the organization is or does – but rather that they are worthy, opaque and written in an obscure and bastardized pseudo-English.

PART II: AID

8. ACTIVE VERSUS PASSIVE WRITING

A common criticism levelled against rookie reporters by frustrated news editors – and an oft-barked order on journalism training courses as a consequence – is that journalists need to inject their writing with 'pace' and 'action'. Put prosaically, those who fail to do so are forgetting that stories should always be about people 'doing something' to other people or things – whether *embracing* them, *racing* them, *criticizing* them, *hitting* them or *fighting* them. Put technically, the prose style of such journalists is too *passive*. Journalism is, after all, almost always concerned with reporting, discussing, debating or reflecting on things that *happen*. To this end, it needs to be *active*.

Let's take as an example a hypothetical local newspaper crime story about an elderly pensioner being robbed of her life savings minutes after withdrawing them from a post office. A passively written intro would relay the information in precisely this order, as follows:

> A 93-year-old pensioner was robbed of her £1,000 life savings by an opportunist thief moments after leaving the bank where she had withdrawn the money.

While the reporter's 'news instinct' is strong here in one respect – he/she has identified that the age (and, arguably, gender) of the crime victim makes her more 'newsworthy' than, say, a fit and active 35-year-old civil servant – by opening the sentence with the attacked, rather than the attacker, he/she has angled it around someone *having something done to them,* rather than *doing something to someone else.* The sentence would be much more active if the reporter instead phrased it as follows:

> An opportunist thief robbed a 93-year-old pensioner of her £1,000 life savings moments after she withdrew the money from her bank.

Here we have a much more 'action-packed' framing of the story. Right at the start of the sentence, our attention is immediately aroused by the presence of the 'opportunist thief' (a crime must have been committed), and the unfolding drama slowly gathers momentum as we read on – with the '93-year-old pensioner' still emerging early on as the robber's victim, the loss of her 'life savings' being detailed soon after, and the intro ending on a punchline with real impact, as it emerges that she had literally only just withdrawn the money from her bank account when she was mugged. Like all good, active, narrative writing, it also sets up a number of questions in our minds that are likely to keep us reading on – a key aim of news-writing (and, indeed, all forms of journalism). For example, was the pensioner hurt during the incident? If so, was she taken to hospital? Did anyone else witness what went on? If so, is there a description of the assailant? Did he or she escape unimpeded? Is the assailant still on the loose, perhaps ready to strike again, or has he or she since been apprehended by the police? Where and when, exactly, did all of this take place?

Hopefully, in this case the virtues of using the active voice in story-telling are self-evident – if nothing else, because of the way this allows the reporter to draw in the reader, by rolling out the key 'who, what, where, when, why, how' aspects of this tale in a controlled but dramatic sequence, punctuated with key details designed to intrigue and ensnare. Thus the revelation about the pensioner's loss of her life savings follows that of her extreme old age and, in turn, the opening gambit about the opportunist thief. A more general way of explaining the importance of active writing, by contrast, is to emphasize its role in conveying the *meaning* of a sentence. Up to now, we have focused on the (very journalistic) concern with 'hooking' readers and persuading them to read on. This is ultimately a function of the commercial nature of most journalism, which is written for mainstream newspapers, magazines and websites whose writers are under pressure from their employers to catch and hold audiences' attention in order to enable the publication to sell advertising and generate profit. But active writing has a purpose much deeper and nobler than to line the pockets of media proprietors (or, indeed, book publishers). It is, quite simply, the best way of informing (and entertaining) the reader, by getting across clearly and concisely what a given sentence, or paragraph, or chapter, or book, is trying to say. Again, the best way to demonstrate this is, as ever, by 'showing':

An example of a passive sentence is this one.

This is an example of an active sentence.

The clues are in the wording (in more ways than one) with each of these two sentences. Of the two, the first is, indeed, 'passive', in that by the time one gets to the end of it, one is struggling to work out (or recall) precisely what it is trying to say. Sentences should not simply be treated as random groups of words thrown together on the page in pretty much any syntactical order. Rather, they need to work as cohesive wholes, with each word following logically and meaningfully after the other, in a sequence which leaves the reader in no doubt about the nature of the point being made and/or information imparted. The first of the aforementioned sentences (though mercifully brief) fails to achieve this end on all counts. The word 'example' lies uselessly near its start, and it ends on the limp term 'this one' – a way of avoiding repeating the word 'sentence' that has the effect of so blunting the point being made by the writer that one is left struggling to remember how he/she began. In the event, the sentence *does* make its point, not by the clarity and punchiness with which it is written but simply by dint of how *passive* it is (this is what I meant by the clue being in the wording earlier on).

By contrast, the second sentence is genuinely active. And the lesson it teaches us about the importance of active writing is, again, much wider and more profound than that we could glean from any made-up story about an assaulted pensioner. Good active sentences *do the work for* the reader, rather than expecting him or her to do it for *them*. Here we have a short, to-the-point statement which conveys, crisply and elegantly, the fact that it is *itself* an example of an active sentence. Contrary to the previous one, it ends with the two most important words it contains: 'active sentence'. There is no need for the reader to scan back over the earlier words in the sentence (as in the passive one) to remind themselves what it is about. Rather, it *ends* on what it is about – in so doing, drumming home the point and giving us a neat sense of closure into the bargain.

Verbs versus Adverbs – When (and When not) to Use Adjectives

Writing actively, rather than passively, does not mean divesting your writing of all colour and description. Although active writing places particular emphasis on the importance of the key building-blocks of sentences – nouns (people or things) and verbs (doing words) – there is still a place for adjectives and adverbs. However, as in novels, short stories and other works of fiction, the more sparingly these are used the greater, invariably, is their impact, and it is for this reason that a 'less is more' approach should generally be adopted when injecting descriptive words into your journalism.

The following are the opening paragraphs of *Hungry for Home* (2000), an award-nominated book by national newspaper journalist Cole Moreton, which chronicles the perilous flight to America of the last families to abandon the remote Great Blasket island off the far west coast of Ireland. It offers a master-class in how to combine active writing with sparse but evocative descriptive flourishes which make no bones about using the odd adjective in the service of a colourful image:

This is the end of the world. The air is full of a terrible wailing. A gale scalps the waves, spilling foam. Gulls shriek as they tumble, caught between the spray, the rain and the low, dark clouds. A mountain stands alone in the sea, its back breaking the wind so that the invisible forces are scattered over its slopes as raiders from the north once were, howling and running down from all directions to the shuttered buildings of a settlement.

A dozen decaying cottages huddle into the hillside, each long and low and built of stone upon stone, each with a bolted door. The wind worries at the roofs, ripping back felt, and animals sheltering in outhouses bellow and moan in fear. This is a wild and lonely place for any living creature, and tonight there is no escape. The island is surrounded, blinded, by a wall of grey cloud, half a mile out in every direction. Behind it, somewhere through the rain and snow, is the mainland, the coast of Corkaguiney, the most westerly tip of Europe. The End of the World, the maps used to say. Beyond be dragons and sea monsters.

'Terrible', 'invisible', 'shuttered', 'decaying', 'wild and lonely' – there is no shortage of adjectives to be found in this passage, and the writing is arguably all the more striking for their presence. But adjectives alone do not a powerful description make: as usual, it is a *combination* of carefully chosen descriptive words and active sentence structure that achieves this. In Moreton's case, this involves a number of literary conceits, not least the use of a technique more familiar from fiction, pathetic fallacy, to personify the elemental forces of nature he describes so eloquently. Hence we read of the gale 'scalping' the waves – a vivid image calling to mind tribal torture – and the wind 'worrying' the roofs, not to mention the island itself being 'blinded' by 'a wall of grey cloud'. Adjectives, then, are a core component of this vivid passage, but they work because they are only used *in the service of* an evocation of the wild and tempestuous scene they are describing. The trick (one that Moreton masters so skilfully) is to avoid any single word drawing too much attention to itself. Words, after all, have no intrinsic value in themselves, but rather are tools for conveying ideas, emotions and meanings – and it is a measure of how careful he is to use them only for this purpose that no one individual word feels showy, intrusive or pretentious. By examining one or two of his choices of adjectives, we can appreciate this point still further. Had Moreton simply described 'a dozen cottages' huddling (more pathetic fallacy) on the hillside, we might have been left with all manner of questions in our minds as we read: for instance, how big or small were the cottages, what colour, what state of repair (or disrepair)? As it is, his precise choice of adjective greatly aids the description, by telling us the cottages are 'decaying' – in so doing, adding to the sense of a battered, besieged community fighting for survival in the wildest of climes. Moreover, it is his use of plain, monosyllabic adjectives (descriptive vocabulary does not need to be florid or complex) to inform us the cottages are 'long and low and built of stone upon stone' that gives us our clearest indication of precisely what they look like.

Used sparingly, then, adjectives can be supremely useful descriptive tools. So, too, can adverbs – or the 'ly' words that describe verbs, adjectives or even other adverbs by conveying the *speed, degree or manner in which* something is being done. Once more, we are entering an area of descriptive prose that can be contentious here: adverbs are notorious for being used gratuitously, and for them to add anything useful or aesthetic to a sentence they need to be deployed selectively and precisely. At the risk of being very post-modern about this, in the sentence before this one I used three adverbs – 'gratuitously', 'selectively' and 'precisely'. Were all of these justified, let alone necessary, or would I have managed to convey the same meaning as effectively, if not more so, by, for example, writing 'overused' instead of 'used gratuitously', and either 'selectively' or 'precisely', as opposed to 'selectively and precisely'? Let the reader be the judge of this, but – in my defence – I chose to write 'used gratuitously' to denote both usages that inject adverbs where none is needed and those that include not one but two or more adverbs where a single one would suffice. I wrote 'selectively and precisely', rather than using just one of the two words, because I was referring to circumstances in which, on the one hand, an adverb was not needed at all (i.e. the need to be selective about when and where to use them) and, on the other, those in which the *wrong* adverb was chosen. Using a clumsy adverb that adds nothing to a sentence's meaning and impact (and may even detract from it) because it is simply the wrong choice of word is arguably as big an error of judgment as introducing one where none is required at all.

Adverbs, then, should only ever be used when they can visibly *add* something to a sentence without which it would feel unfinished or imprecise. The words of primary importance in any sentence, though, are those active building-blocks – the nouns and verbs – and it is often the case that anything an adverb can add could be conveyed more effectively by spending a little more time choosing a better verb. Put differently, if a verb seems to 'need' an adverb to clarify its meaning, or lend it impact, then it might well be that you have not chosen the 'right' (or most descriptive) verb in the first place, and your first stop should be to search for synonyms in a thesaurus, rather than needlessly add more words to your sentence. Imagine, for example, you are writing a description of a tense encounter between two people, and are trying to get across the level of anger or hatred with which one of the two parties looks at the other. You might write that this person 'stared piercingly' at the other – justifying the adverb by reflecting that, had you omitted it, the reader would have been none the wiser about how menacing or disdainful was the look cast. An alternative approach, however, might have been to replace the words 'stared piercingly' with 'glared': in other words, by refining your choice of verb (replacing the more neutral 'stared' with the more aggressive 'glared'), you would have both obviated the need for an adverb and conveyed your point with more impact. This is not always the case, though – and (as with adjectives) a well-chosen adverb will sometimes enhance the meaning of a sentence in a way no amount of fine-tuning your verb choices can achieve. For instance, if you were to write that the second of your two protagonists 'stared *pleadingly*' at the first, you would be communicating a sense of vulnerability and victimhood much more effectively than if you were to leave it simply as 'stared' – or, for that matter, any obvious synonym for that word. In this case, a well-judged adverb would have served to lend the sentence genuine meaning and value.

At the risk of labouring the point, here is a short extract from *Bring Home the Revolution: The Case for a British Republic*, a 1998 book by *Guardian* journalist Jonathan Freedland. In it, he is describing what he calls a 'normal family' – something he invites the reader to interpret as a reference to the kind of wholesome, 'all-American', nuclear household familiar from any number of advertising hoardings and media portrayals. Although Freedland goes on to end with a cunning punchline, as in all good dropped intros, it transpires that he is actually referring to residents of a *place* called Normal, as opposed to an 'average' or 'typical' family, in its opening paragraph – he is clearly playing for effect on a well-worn white, middle-income, middle-American stereotype. And the single adverb he uses to help him convey one of the passage's most arresting images is arguably not only justified, but necessary:

> The Normal family has four members. Father is strong with broad shoulders, mother has long, flowing hair. They sit close, while their two children – a boy and a girl – sprawl lovingly across their laps. They are fit, smiling and white.

The use of the word 'lovingly' here adds real meaning. If the verb 'sprawl' had been used in isolation it could have signified any of a number of things. Are we to take it, for instance, that the kids are asleep? By adding the word 'lovingly', though, Freedland is helping us visualize something very different: nothing less than the saccharine, idealized image of the 'perfect' family unit, all smiles, embraces and mutual understanding. More importantly, in the context of this particular chapter, he is imbuing the children with *agency*. Far from being passive objects – the *recipients* of their parents' love and protection – they are actively contributing to an *exchange* of emotions, by (presumably) smiling and directing positive body language towards their mother and father in a gesture of affection. Far from being superfluous or redundant, then, the adverb is here a crucial fixture of the sentence, without which the image the writer is striving for would have been that much more elusive.

Structuring Sentences and Prioritizing Information

Although judging when and how to use – and, more often, *not* use – descriptive words is a key 'trick of the trade' in active writing, as the earlier illustrations about the dangers of passive sentence structures highlighted, perhaps the most vital skill is an ability to identify the best *order* in which to lay down information. In news-writing (as Chapter 1 emphasized), the particular onus placed on reporters to 'grab' readers within the space of the first twenty-five words or so means that ill-judged syntax or sequencing can be potentially fatal: quite simply, you have a matter of seconds to hook them and, if you fail to do so, the casual browser will already have flipped pages or clicked onto another article (or even site). For the journalist who has spent hours or days diligently investigating a story, only for readers' eyes to pass over it uninterested for want of a catchy enough intro, this can be a cause of intense professional frustration. For editors and media proprietors, in today's ever-more bottom line-driven digital environment, it can mean the difference between holding readers' attention and engaging them in discussion and debate (in so doing, giving advertisers more exposure) and losing them entirely to a rival publication they can access with a single, impatient click of their mouse.

Framing sentences in a way designed to maximize their impact is, then, an especially vital part of the process of fashioning the *intros* to articles. But how do the general lessons we have already covered about active writing translate into a day-to-day 'rule-book' that can be applied, automatically and without too much thought, to the nitty-gritty of 'constructing' intros? Firstly, there is much to be said for the simple lesson that it is not just the overall choice of what to put in an intro that is important, but the order in which those ingredients are included. To take the fictional example used earlier to highlight the importance of active writing in news stories, the inclusion of the 'opportunist thief' so near the start, or 'front', of the sentence is a deliberate ploy designed to halt the casual reader in his or her tracks. After this point, it is important to progress quickly from the 'who' element of the intro to the 'what' (and, by extension, 'to whom') – i.e. the theft of the pensioner's life savings. The *sequence*, then, in which the facts of the story are set out – with all the most significant (and interesting) information frontloaded as early as possible – is a key aspect of both the active writing process and the hardwired commercial drive to grab readers in which many journalists are (however reluctantly) engaged.

Though the need to prioritize information is especially evident in the process of crafting intros for news stories, the same could be said for any introductory sentence or paragraph – from the scene-setting openings of features and profiles to the crucial 'make-or-break' first pages of far lengthier forms of journalism, including books. In fact, in many ways, the risk of failing to hook readers at the start of a book – a far lengthier investment of their time and energy than any kind of article – is much greater. For this reason, however much space a book allows for its writer to develop his or her ideas slowly over a number of chapters, in its opening paragraph it needs to work hard to catch and hold its readers' attention. This does not, however, mean that (like news stories) it must deliver all the goods upfront: rather, like the more playful openings of many longer features, it is often possible to combine active sentence construction with an imaginative and lateral overall intro structure more reminiscent of the 'dropped' intro than the 'straight' one. By way of illustration, the following is the opening gambit of *The Last Party*, music journalist John Harris's celebrated 2003 history of the 'Britpop' era of popular music:

> For most of the 80s, the UK remained stuck in one cultural moment. Its one-woman wellspring was in Downing Street from 1979 to 1990; such was the impact of her governments on every fibre of British life that she gave rise not only to an 'ism', but a fully-fledged era.

Notwithstanding Harris's use of an erroneous hyphen after the adverb 'fully' (we'll forgive him that), this initial paragraph is an example of how a seasoned 'dropped intro-writer' might usefully import this skill into the act of book-writing. To focus on its 'active' qualities first, the paragraph begins with a short sentence designed to tease the reader into proceeding further. Rather than lodging the term 'one cultural moment' (or similar) somewhere in its middle, Harris deliberately opts to end his sentence with it – thereby serving up something concrete yet intriguing with which to entice readers onwards. For anyone of a certain age who had lived through the 1980s in Britain (a seismic period, socially and economically, as Harris's book goes on to reflect), the words 'one cultural moment' are likely to conjure up at least an oblique idea of the kind of (political) 'culture' to which he refers. For anyone else, though – particularly those attracted to the book less by its background socio-political context than the prospect of learning more about the bands of the then-recent Britpop era – it serves the purpose of injecting an element of mystery, even mischief, that may well draw them in. As with any dropped intro worth its salt, though, Harris is still teasing us somewhat by the time we reach the end of his second sentence. While it would take a total political refusenik (or ignoramus) not to have worked out by this point that he is referring to Margaret Thatcher, nowhere in the whole paragraph is she mentioned by name. A fusion of active writing and the slow-burn, 'egg them on' approach of the delayed drop, then, can prove a highly effective way of 'setting up' a lengthy piece of journalism – just as far shorter items require journalists to hit the ground running from the word go.

There is, though, a further lesson to be drawn from this focus on the order, or sequencing, of words in written journalism. For individual sentences (and paragraphs) to deliver the required punch, they need to not only be actively written in the broadest sense, but also to *begin and end* with solid, impactful information (and, ideally, incident). And, if they can include plenty more of that at strategic points in between, then so much the better. In the previous example, Harris arguably achieves this by opening with his 'most of the 80s' and culminating, in a nicely rounded way, with the term 'fully-fledged era' (a reference, of course, to that very same decade). Between these two points he has introduced us to his key theme – the aforementioned 'one cultural moment' – and, indirectly, the main protagonist who shaped it (Thatcher) and the political 'philosophy' she spawned (Thatcherism). In so doing, Harris is borrowing from the hand-book 'written' (if not literally) many years previously by pioneers like Orwell, as they put pen to paper to describe very different times – albeit with the same eye to the impact of politics, and war, on the wider cultural landscape. In 'England Your England', his classic 1941 exploration of the nature of patriotism at a time of global conflict, Orwell began with the following:

> As I write, highly civilized human beings are flying over-head, trying to kill me.
>
> (George Orwell, The Lion and the Unicorn: Socialism and the
> English Genius, HarperCollins, 1941)

This single fourteen-word sentence constituted his entire opening paragraph, and though few contemporary readers can have doubted what it was referring to (the pilots of Germany's Luftwaffe), at no point does he explicitly say this. Indeed, compared to Harris's (lengthier) opener, with its comparatively laboured references to Thatcher, he throws us tantalizingly few scraps of information on which to base our interpretation of precisely what is going on. Can the 'highly civilized human beings' he mentions at the outset *really* be members of the enemy's air force – those responsible for carpet-bombing large swathes of our cities, killing innocent civilians, and leaving numerous families homeless? Or, given the title of the essay, is he not referring to *our own* (brave) forces? If so, what can he mean by suggesting they are 'trying to kill' him? Of course, these and other mysteries swiftly unravel as the reader presses on, but Orwell's stark juxtaposition of the opening image of 'civilized human beings' and the (equally solid) closing one of himself facing dire peril at their hands acts as an object lesson in both journalistic sequencing and tight, impact-heavy active writing.

Paragraphing and Signposting

Order and sequence are not, of course, important solely in the context of structuring individual sentences or paragraphs. For articles, essays or books to work, they must introduce their themes, characters and ideas in logical succession, and for this reason ensuring that one paragraph flows 'naturally' on from another is vital to keeping your audience with you and giving them the best value possible in your journalism. In many respects, the principles underpinning the choices you make about what information to include (and where), and which words to use (and in what order) in an individual sentence or paragraph are much the same when you come to structuring and paragraphing an entire piece. Above all else, you are trying to avoid what are known as *non sequiturs* – or sudden 'jolts', 'jumps' or 'gaps' in an unfolding narrative which break the link between one scene or action and the next, in so doing raising unintended questions about how a character got 'from A to B' or 'one thing led to another'. Nonetheless, keeping the momentum going for an article spread over 3,000 words or (in the case of Orwell) twenty-eight pages – let alone the length of a whole book – is undeniably challenging. Rather than merely worrying about keeping an individual passage pacey and involving, paragraphing is about making sure that an *entire text* is active, from start to finish. By methodically applying the same rules about active voice and sequencing, though, and using these to guide you step by step through the process, you should find the task becomes increasingly easy with practice.

The business of crafting an active, logically sequenced piece differs, in certain respects, from one form of journalism to another. As Chapter 1 stressed, news stories are structured very differently to other forms of writing, and with a much more prescriptive formula which places primary emphasis on the 'who, what, where, when, why, how' elements of the immediate angle: i.e. what happened last night or this morning to whom, and how and where it took place? This information is frontloaded in the intro, and from this point the reporter initially goes back over each element of the intro 'angle' (or nub of the story), fleshing out the detail to fill in gaps in the reader's knowledge left by the necessarily sketchy opening sentence (or sentences). In other words, the sequencing, or paragraphing, of news stories is inherently distinct from any kind of writing (journalism included) that follows a more linear, or chronological, progression – including many features. Within the confines of its own particular 'rule-book', though, the very fact that news is so rigidly structured – with quotes following the first three paragraphs and historical background left until much lower down – means it works to an even more clearly defined paragraphing 'logic'. Combined with the enforced brevity of its form, this makes it comparatively easy to sequence news when set against other, lengthier types of assignment, as the inverted pyramid straitjacket affords reporters far less choice than, say, feature-writers or essayists about which details to include, and in what order. It would be untrue to say, though, that there are no aspects of news-writing in which paragraphing is approached in a similar way to how it is in other types of journalism. In the sequencing of the story at the core of a written news report, the central account of 'who has done what to whom' should be relayed in precisely that order: i.e. rather like the slow-motion 'action-replays' familiar from television football match reports or the dramatic reconstructions staged for TV crime programmes. This one aspect of news-writing must be reported in a linear, or chronological, way if the final article is to accurately reflect the exact order in which an event or incident unfolded, or the context in which a speech was delivered or an argument broke out.

This being said, it is primarily in the context of longer-form journalism that the challenge of effective paragraphing becomes most acute. How, then, should the feature-writer or essayist rise to this challenge? One way of conceiving of your 'route-map' through an article is to return to some of the principles outlined in Chapter 2, which explored the conventions of feature-writing. If you think of yourself as a guide leading your readers through a topic or issue – or, in the case of some reportage and travelogue-writing, perhaps even on an actual journey you have taken yourself while researching your article – you are unlikely to go far wrong. What each successive paragraph needs to do is nudge, or lure, your readers ever onwards, while also rewarding their perseverance to this point by introducing the next development, twist or revelation. Effective paragraphing is about structuring a coherent and compelling overall *narrative*, in much the same way as the best novelists lead us tantalizingly from one plot point to another. Metaphorically speaking, your narrative can be likened to a colourful, intricately patterned tapestry or carpet you are slowly unrolling for the reader to (eventually) view in all its glory. Another analogy – to which we will return in the next section, as we explore the need for journalists to write 'visually' – might be that of a movie. Most films are 'storyboarded' in a clear narrative sequence, which ensures that one scene follows logically and coherently on from another – and, for example, characters do not magically appear and disappear at random points, but rather are introduced to viewers properly when they first appear and thereafter re-enter the story for meaningful reasons at specific junctures. Barring various subgenres that make a virtue out of using flashbacks and adopting a 'jigsaw' approach to story-telling (some more successfully than others), if a movie fails to make sure its viewers can keep up with what is going on – by extension, holding their interest – it has failed. Similarly, if longer-form journalists were to skip to the later details, or conclusions, of their articles too soon, they would run the risk of 'losing' their readers, by neglecting to take them, logically and progressively, through the sequence of narrative threads or frames that 'lead' to that point. Put more commercially, if they were to 'give everything away' near the start, or a third of the way through, what incentive would readers have to continue reading to the end – or advertisers to pay for print space or online page-views when they had failed to do so?

The fact that we are talking here, largely, about longer articles and books makes it practically impossible to illustrate these points in any detail. Doing so would require us to examine a long extract which demonstrates the logical sequencing of paragraphs over several thousand words or a large number of pages. However, one or two shorter examples, taken from the middle of extended pieces of journalism, should suffice to illustrate the basic principles of narrative flow in journalistic paragraphing. Our first extract is from a 2001 *Guardian* feature by cult freelance journalist Jon Ronson, in which he chronicles the year he spent following the fortunes of the first set of contestants to enter the then-popular Channel 4 reality show *Big Brother* – following the end of their 'five minutes of fame' on television. In it Ronson repeatedly teases his readers with a studiedly sequential series of witty anecdotes which leads them on an odyssey through the ups and downs of minor 'celebrities' as they struggle to come to terms (some more successfully than others) with their return to everyday life. The extract, taken from the last third of the 2,600-word feature (the first of a two-parter), begins with the publicist employed by most of the ex-contestants to keep up their profiles advising Ronson to meet Andy Davidson, whom he describes as having 'adjusted' best of all to his old life. It ends with a very different image: that of Andy refusing to return to nine-to-five working, in preference for an ersatz showbiz lifestyle he is now largely experiencing vicariously through better-known fellow contestants:

> 'Andy is great,' said Keith. 'Andy has adjusted well to life beyond Big Brother. You'll like him. You really should meet him. When are you free?'
>
> So my meeting with Andy was Keith's way of proving to me that Endemol could not be held responsible for the self-destructive behaviour displayed by other housemates. Keith was effectively saying, 'Look at Andy. Andy's okay. See? It isn't our fault.'
>
> Andy and I entered the offices of Courier Systems. 'This is wicked,' said Andy. 'I've always wanted to be a cycle courier.'
>
> (Jon Ronson, 'Stars in their eyes (part one)', www.guardian.co.uk,
> 7 July 2001)

This sets the article up well for the unfolding farce, when the supposedly modest, down-to-earth Andy takes up and quits a cycle courier job within the space of a few short lines:

'When can you start?' said Paul, the manager.

'Tomorrow,' said Andy. 'Bright and early.'

Paul laughed. He said he'd seen people like Andy before. They come in full of excitement and fanciful ideals about the life of the cycle courier, but reality hits them on the first day and they quit within a week.

'Well, that's not me,' said Andy. 'I promise you that.'

'Will I see you at Sada's [fellow contestant] book launch party?' I asked.

'No,' he said. 'I'm not going.'

'Why not?' I asked.

'It would be deceitful,' he said. 'I fucking hate Sada.'

(Ibid.)

Even now, though, the real punchline is to come, as Ronson delivers a deadpan account of Andy's double volte-face – his pathetically short stint as a courier, and decision to renege on his earlier pledge not to be seen dead at Sada's book launch:

Andy's career as a cycle courier lasted for three days.

'God it was hard,' he told me at Sada's book launch party. 'And the money was shit. And then last Friday I was having a great day talking to all these journalists and my phone rang and this angry voice said, "It's Paul from the office." And I thought, "What fucking office?" And he starts yelling, "Friday is our busiest day! Why aren't you working?" Jesus! So I quit.'

The impact of Ronson's wit can be put down, in no small part, to the heroic understatement of his writing. Ask yourself how much less effective – and how much more crass and spiteful – it would have been if he had simply launched into an attack on Andy's delusions of grandeur, or simply 'told' us he was egotistical, rather than 'showing' us the extent of his vanity in such an identifiable and amusing way. So naturalistic are the exchanges between Ronson and Keith the publicist, Andy and the courier company boss and Ronson and Andy that we are all-but transported into the room(s) with them. More than this: if we are honest with ourselves, we can almost imagine being in Andy's shoes, clinging to our last gasp of fame even as the hard reality of earning a living when the VIP passes dry up and the phone stops ringing hits home. But the sharpness of Ronson's satire rests not only on the effortless, un-showy texture of his writing or his instinctive ear for dialogue but his eye for the importance of *sequence*: Andy's ignominious 'fall from grace' would not have worked nearly as well on the page if we had not been led through it, step by step, from the mundanity of his interview for the courier job to his 'surprise' appearance at the 'hated' Sada's launch.

What Ronson also shows us throughout his article – not least in the above extract – is the importance of narrative *signposting*. This is a device considered vital to novelists, dramatists and other forms of narrative-writer concerned with keeping their readers on board through long stretches of text – and, equally crucially, rewarding those who pay attention with little 'bonuses' that will add to their appreciation of the work. Though his signposts are hardly subliminal, Ronson scatters them throughout this passage. They are there in the opening remark from Keith assuring him about Andy's grounded personality and, particularly, the jaded comments from Paul (his short-lived 'boss') about other wannabe couriers who 'quit within a week' – claims comprehensively dismantled and vindicated respectively in ensuing paragraphs, which culminate in the image of a champagne-swilling Andy complaining about being interrupted by a call from work while he was 'talking to all these journalists'.

Let us close this chapter by looking at one other, more sustained and subtle, example of journalistic signposting. In his 2002 memoir, *Give Me Ten Seconds*, former ITN political editor John Sergeant opens by recalling the time when, as a more junior correspondent for the BBC, he (unwittingly) scooped his broadcast rivals by clumsily careering, microphone in hand, into then-Prime Minister Mrs Thatcher as she emerged from Number 10 Downing Street to announce her intention to continue fighting for the Conservative Party leadership after being challenged by former colleague Michael Heseltine. This anecdote – already well-rehearsed at the time the book came out as the fabled occasion when the former premier 'handbagged' Sergeant – initially appears to have been employed as little more than a cheap hook designed to strike a familiar chord with readers. However, as the book progresses, and Sergeant rewinds over the next few chapters to recount his earlier life and (pre-handbagging) career, it becomes clear it is actually being used as a clever narrative thread to tie together the early sections with strands that are to follow much later. In particular, through the prism of Thatcher's fight for survival, and her ensuing resignation, a cast of characters is introduced who will return to dominate the last quarter of the book – all of whom had become key political players by the time Sergeant found himself at the peak of his broadcasting career. These include Thatcher's eventual successor, John Major, Heseltine himself and the collective noun 'New Labour', which would return in the penultimate chapter in the guise of its leading players, Tony Blair and Peter Mandelson. Signposts, then, can be used not only to send echoes bouncing around the text, or reverberating from one chapter to another, but as an overall framing device to bind together the entire piece of writing.

9. WRITING VISUALLY

If writing 'actively' ought to be a hardwired instinct in journalists, so, too, should the need to think (and write) *visually*. Much of the first section of this book is concerned with types of journalism that involve thinking, and writing, more deeply, reflectively and/or descriptively than the simple 'five Ws' straitjacket of a short news story allows (or requires). Yet even news, at its best, is highly visual, in terms of the clarity of the verbs and nouns used to convey it. The invented example used earlier of the '93-year-old pensioner' having her 'life savings' stolen by an 'opportunist thief' evokes, in its own limited way, a strong image. If the reporter were to add that the robber(s) had 'left' the poor woman 'for dead' after 'beating her over the head with a baseball bat', the story would be rendered yet more dramatic and shocking – not just because of the *details* of what had transpired, but because of the clipped, no-nonsense way in which they were relayed to us. Contrast this active, 'someone doing something to someone else' approach – reliant purely on verbs ('doing words') and nouns ('things') – with a more wordy take on the story. Had the reporter used twice as many words to get across the same events, or added layers of description, the intro might well have lost its immediate visual impact, rather than gaining from the addition of adverbs and adjectives. Would the writer really have brought the incident to life more by telling us the victim was a 'frail 93-year-old pensioner', as opposed to simply a '93-year-old pensioner'? Surely to add this adjective would be tantamount to stating the obvious. Indeed, if the woman were not frail, at such a senior age, we might well be looking at a very different kind of story! Similarly, would the writer have been adding any more visual impact by stating that the robbers 'violently' beat the pensioner with a baseball bat? Put simply, what might add value to the mix in fiction – or, indeed, longer-form journalism – can very often detract from the necessary immediacy required of 'wham, bam' news reports.

But what *of* those longer-form pieces of journalism? How far should journalists go in using language to flesh out, and add visual flourishes, to their features and reportage? When does journalistic writing *benefit* from the addition of more colour and texture to help readers visualize a place, incident or person – and under what circumstances, even in longer articles, does understatement still win out?

As ever with journalistic writing, it is a question of achieving the right balance. Verbs and nouns might be the most effective way of conveying an immediate mental picture of a news event, but adjectives and (to a lesser extent) adverbs have their place when it comes to adding lustre to a scene we want to describe more tangibly. In Chapter 2 we considered the advantages of carrying out interviews face to face, rather than over the phone or social media – and most of these, in prose terms, related to the need to 'bring to life' the subject, by not merely relating what they *say* but describing their tone of voice, appearance, mood, or how relaxed, flustered, tired or energetic they seem. Verbs and nouns help us communicate these qualities, of course – if one were to write that a famous singer 'croaked his way through the interview', for instance, one would both be writing actively and conveying the fact that, unusually, he was struggling with his voice. But elsewhere in the interview it might benefit the feature if we were to gently 'remind' readers of this fact, by stating that he 'replies hoarsely' (note the adverb), rather than simply dusting off the word 'croaked' (or a direct variation thereof) and using it again. If nothing else, using the word 'hoarsely' on the second mention of the singer's 'lost' voice would have avoided the need for repetition. And *varying* one's vocabulary, by using synonyms or finding different ways of phrasing a similar point or idea, is arguably another key lesson of which journalists – especially those writing lengthier articles – should be mindful.

The same latitude applies, in more lengthy pieces, to adjectives. If our singer appeared relaxed when we met him – and we felt conveying this fact to readers would add value or meaning to their appreciation of the article – we might state precisely this: i.e. that he 'appeared' or 'looked relaxed'. But is this really writing visually, in the truest sense of the term, or merely 'telling' readers something, rather than 'showing' them? After all, we are expecting them to trust our judgement (from our eyewitness vantage-point) (a) that he *did*, indeed, look relaxed and (b) that aspects of his manner and appearance we interpreted as signs of relaxation are the same as those *they* would view in this way. Far better to describe him as wearing an 'unbuttoned shirt and ripped jeans' – an image of casual nonchalance that relies purely on the journalist's (literal) description of what he or she sees, rather than value judgements about what those signifiers 'say' about the subject's frame of mind. In either case, though, the writer would be relying, at least in part, on the use of adjectives (whether 'relaxed' or 'unbuttoned' and 'ripped') to help create the reader's mental image of the singer's mode of dress and accompanying demeanour.

The following is an extract from *Guardian* feature-writer Andy Beckett's critically acclaimed revisionist history of the political turmoil of 1970s Britain, *When the Lights Went Out* (2009). One of the standout qualities of this book is that, unlike many other popular histories, including those by other journalists, such as the BBC's Andrew Marr, Beckett brings to his account not only a keen awareness of the historical context of the times about which he is writing (though he is scarcely old enough to remember it personally) but also a real journalistic sensibility. Far from merely collating information and drawing out inferences from secondary sources, he weaves in his own first-hand research, including fragments of interviews with key players in his narrative that he either conducted for the book itself or some years previously, while working on other assignments. In this particular excerpt Beckett introduces us to Jack Jones, erstwhile general secretary of the former Transport and General Workers'

Union (TGWU). Though sparing in his choice of prose, in a single paragraph he conjures up a vivid portrait of this proud, once-confrontational, union man:

> At ninety-one, his persona was little changed. The TGWU headquarters had moved from Smith Square to Holborn, further from the centre of power, and was housed in an anonymous modern office block with corporations as neighbours. But Jones sat behind a desk, arms folded and watchful, in the corner office he still used several days a week as chairman of the National Pensioners Convention, an organization he had set up for retired trade unionists. He wore a blue suit and waistcoat, and looked about seventy. His cloth cap hung from the coat stand. A plaque commemorating the service of Liverpudlians in the Spanish Civil War hung from the wall. A sense that his life was part of an ongoing, age-old struggle lingered strongly in the room.

Though far from flawless (whose writing is?), this passage is packed with biographical colour, which adds welcome personality to a chapter that, up to this point, has been engaged in a breakneck exposition designed to bring readers unfamiliar with Jones 'up to speed' with his turbulent years as a union leader. Beckett achieves much of this by using verbs and nouns alone: we find Jones 'sat behind a desk', his 'arms folded', and wearing a 'blue suit and waistcoat' (the latter phrase guilty of only the most literal adjectival usage). But how much more Beckett's character sketch gains, arguably, through his use of the adjective 'watchful' to interpret the guarded manner Jones projects, and his description of the 'anonymous' office block in which the union is now based. The passage is full of pathos, too – in particular, a sense both of Jones's enduring dedication to his life's cause but also of the mighty having fallen. For those paying close attention to one of the book's underlying currents (the sense that the 1970s, to paraphrase L.P. Hartley's novel *The Go-Between*, was a foreign country), Beckett's reference to the 'corporations' with whom Jones now shares premises, and his being shunted 'further from the centre of power' – Smith Square being located in Westminster, the heart of the political establishment, Holborn in the City of London financial district – adds to the sense that Jones symbolizes a breed of influential unionists who have had their day. Even Beckett's rather heavy-handed reference to his 'sense' of an 'ongoing, age-old struggle' lingering 'strongly' in the room (perhaps an adverb too many) is arguably justified by the fact that, if we are still reading by this stage in the book, it is a fair assumption that our narrator's judgement thus far has earned our trust.

The Use of Filmic Imagery

We explored the importance of sequencing words and information in the last chapter. Just as journalists should always try to think, and therefore write, visually in general terms – using vivid prose to paint mental pictures for their readers – so, too, should their writing relay *events*, *actions* and *processes* like a film or newsreel, using active language, carefully ordered, to convey an impression of dynamism and activity. But this is not the only way in which the process of journalistic storytelling can be likened to directing a movie or composing frames as a cinematographer.

If we were to use a cinematic analogy to describe the previous extract, we might liken it to an establishing shot. Beckett is panning around Jones's office, carefully picking out the fixtures and furnishings that signify something about him: his 'desk', his 'cloth cap', the 'plaque' on the wall. He has pulled back the camera and is framing Jones, 'arms folded and watchful', against the backdrop of his native habitat – a dinosaur from another age sitting guard in its lair.

The 'establishing shot' approach to journalistic narratives can be highly effective (as it is here), and for this reason offers a useful way to 'break in' to a feature, colour piece or book. As the old saying goes, 'a picture is worth a thousand words': a journalistic picture, framed by a master story-teller and wordsmith with an eye for an arresting establishing shot, maybe more so.

10. LIMITING THE FIRST PERSON

ONE OF THE MOST contentious questions in modern journalism is when, if at all, writers are justified in using the *first person*. Although certain articles – reviews, comment pieces and opinion columns spring to mind – not only permit a certain amount of personal input from the writer, but demand it, others most certainly do not. Indeed, with news stories, features, reportage and almost all other forms of journalistic writing, it is a truth (almost) universally acknowledged that the one thing journalists should *not* be in the business of doing is making *themselves* the subject of their articles. Journalists are there to bear witness to (and chronicle) important events, people, things and places: it is not their place to elevate themselves to a status comparable to, let alone greater than, the subjects about which they are meant to be writing.

This being said, there are times when the very business of 'bearing witness' more than justifies the use of 'I' and 'me'. For instance, if a journalist were fortunate (or unfortunate) enough to find him/herself in a unique or privileged situation – caught up in the midst of a spontaneous demonstration or running for cover as a bomb blast hit a crowded shopping-centre – it would be a missed opportunity if his/her editor did not commission a first-person colour piece, perhaps one explicitly conveying the fear, alarm or other emotions the journalist experienced as the drama unfolded. The following extract is taken from a 1993 interview by *The Independent*'s veteran Middle

173

East correspondent, Robert Fisk, with the man who, nine years later, would become the world's most wanted terrorist: Osama bin Laden. It is a startling example of how reports from distant places the public are being invited to take on trust can gain a sense of authenticity and immediacy from the use of a first-person narrative. But although Fisk does use 'I' in places, even in the context of an exclusive encounter with this seldom-interviewed, enigmatic and almost mystical individual, he does so only three times in more than 1,000 words – and it is a full eleven paragraphs before the first instance of it appears. Understatement, as ever, wins out, and the article is all the more vivid and intimate because of this:

> OSAMA Bin Laden sat in his gold-fringed robe, guarded by the loyal Arab mujahedin who fought alongside him in Afghanistan. Bearded, taciturn figures – unarmed, but never more than a few yards from the man who recruited them, trained them and then dispatched them to destroy the Soviet army – they watched unsmiling as the Sudanese villagers of Almatig lined up to thank the Saudi businessman who is about to complete the highway linking their homes to Khartoum for the first time in history.
>
> With his high cheekbones, narrow eyes and long brown robe, Mr Bin Laden looks every inch the mountain warrior of mujahedin legend. Chadored children danced in front of him, preachers acknowledged his wisdom. 'We have been waiting for this road through all the revolutions in Sudan,' *a sheikh said*. 'We waited until we had given up on everybody – and then Osama Bin Laden came along.'
>
> (Robert Fisk, 'Anti-Soviet warrior puts his army on the road to peace: The Saudi businessman who recruited mujahedin now uses them for large-scale building projects in Sudan', *The Independent*, 6 December 1993)

When the first person does finally show itself, it is in the context of a question Fisk puts to bin Laden that would arguably have been difficult for him to convey on the page in any other way. Pressing him on the question of how many of his fellow 'mujahedin' he had helped flee to Sudan from Afghanistan after their successful banishment of Soviet troops from that country – and in an effort to coax from him an admission of his involvement in conflicts involving Muslims elsewhere – Fisk writes:

> How many? Osama Bin Laden shakes his head. 'I don't want to say. But they are here now with me, they are working right here, building this road to Port Sudan.' I told him that Bosnian Muslim fighters in the Bosnian town of Travnik had mentioned his name to me. 'I feel the same about Bosnia,' he said. 'But the situation there does not provide the same opportunities as Afghanistan. A small number of mujahedin have gone to fight in Bosnia-Herzegovina but the Croats won't allow the mujahedin in through Croatia as the Pakistanis did with Afghanistan.'
>
> (Ibid.)

Even when the first person *is* justified as a narrative tool for drawing readers in to a scenario or otherwise bringing it to life, it is still best to use it sparingly, and in a highly focused way. At no point is Fisk in danger of letting his own vanity intrude in the telling of his story: his presence in the room is subordinated to that of his subject (bin Laden) throughout, rather than the other way round. This is exactly as it should be. Contrast this approach with the following excerpt from a sprawling 3,500-word feature written by novelist Melanie McGrath for the first issue of *Tate Magazine* in 2002. Billed as an interview with another elusive figure, the artist Tracey Emin, it contains only a single direct quote from its subject (hardly evidence of an encounter at all) and opens with a lengthy, elliptical and self-indulgent preamble which places the interviewer, rather than the interviewee, centre-stage:

> I've never given Tracey Emin much real thought. Until a few weeks ago I passed her off as the artist who displayed her bed in the Tate and lurched about pissed on TV. I'm of a mind to blame celebrity for this, because of course Tracey Emin is a celebrity. A big one. The kind who only has to

sneeze to make it into the red tops. I'm not immune to her fame. I've had my fair share of celebrity thoughts about her. They're not all that interesting. Here are some: 'She looks like Frida Kahlo', and 'I wonder what she'd be like in bed?' and 'She must be worth a bloody bomb' (I did warn you). But as for real live-and-kicking ideas, actual neural sparks, genuine considered opinions about Emin as an artist, well, they have been a bit thin on my intellectual ground.

So here's where I begin. These thoughts aren't entirely worked out yet. I'm still in a process of discovery. But then you probably are too. So what you're about to read is a sort of travelogue of ideas, a trip across my mind as it considers Tracey Emin. You'll add in your thoughts and feelings and if we're lucky we'll get somewhere by the end.

My first thought isn't very out of the ordinary. You might have had it too. In fact, if you're reading this, you probably have. It's this:

'I don't know whether Tracey Emin is a great artist.'

(Melanie McGrath, 'Something's wrong', *Tate Magazine*,
1 October 2002)

Trying Things Out – Other Justifications for the First Person

The other form of reporting (and, more often, feature-writing) which most justifies the use of a first-person perspective is the 'experiential' article: for instance, a 'how-to' piece exploring a new craze or pastime. In such cases, the role of the reporter or feature-writer becomes more akin to that of a reviewer, in some respects, as they try their hand at a bizarre new extreme sport, strut their stuff on the catwalk, or climb Mount Everest – and emerge from the experience to tell us what it was like.

In general terms, though, it is advisable to approach the first person with caution. Although it has recently seen a minor renaissance in magazines and supplements (with something approaching a full-blown revival in America), this has largely been in the context of a new breed of 'confessional' articles. Often (though by no means always) written by guest contributors, rather than regular staff journalists, these typically focus on issues and experiences relating to the rigours and challenges of modern life – from the difficulties of juggling work with family commitments to personal experiences of relationships, crime, bereavement or serious illness. Germaine Greer, Suzanne Moore and Julie Burchill are among those adept at the newspaper confessional, with the latter using her columns on a succession of titles to chronicle almost every aspect of her colourful love life. In the following extract, Deborah Orr uses her own *Guardian* column to announce her diagnosis with cancer, and to take this peg as a springboard to launch into a list of '10 things you should never, ever say to someone when they're ill':

> The biggest shock, when I was diagnosed with cancer the summer before last, was quickly observing that people can be quite competitive in their determination to 'be there for you', and occasionally unable to hide their chagrin when some other chum has been awarded a particularly sensitive role at a particularly sensitive medical consultation. Nobody means to be intrusive or irritating. It's all done with the finest intentions. But, God, it's a pain.
>
> (Deborah Orr, '10 things not to say to someone when they're ill',
> *The Guardian*, 18 April 2012)

Whether you find this mode of highly personalized journalism effective, or affecting, is very much a matter of taste (at the risk of veering into the first person myself, it has never 'worked' for this writer!). However, that it is becoming increasingly commonplace and popular is demonstrably true – with most of the biggest-selling magazines, from *Cosmopolitan* to *Good Housekeeping* to *Take a Break*, running confessional pieces (frequently contributed by readers) in more or less every issue. And, while it might have been possible for at least some of these articles to be penned equally effectively, if not more so, by journalists using the third person, it is undoubtedly true that a first-person account of, say, a violent marriage or the death of a child by someone who has

experienced it directly – whether they happen to be a journalist or a reader – can, if well edited and positioned, prove very
powerful.

How to 'Get Personal' While *Avoiding* 'I' and 'me'

Many columnists routinely use the first person. In recent years,
red-top and mid-market tabloids in particular have repeatedly
employed celebrity writers to fill these positions – from break-
fast TV host Lorraine Kelly in *The Sun* and husband-and-wife
presenting team Richard Madeley and Judy Finnigan in the
Daily Express to one-time *Daily Mirror* film critic Jonathan Ross.
Part of the appeal of these regular columns – at least as much
as the wisdom dispensed in them – rests on the popularity of
the columnist (which usually relates more to whatever it is
they do outside journalism than anything they write within
it). Controversialists like the *Daily Mail*'s Melanie Phillips and
Richard Littlejohn or *Evening Standard* art critic Brian Sewell,
meanwhile, are professional journalists who have built up such
high profiles that they have become celebrities in their own right
– and the main attraction of their columns rests on the forth-
right, unvarnished views they habitually express.

With large picture by-lines bestriding their pages, it is hardly
surprising that such 'star' columnists get away with liberal
sprinklings of 'I' and 'me', and arguably their ranting and raving
would not be the same without this. But not *all* articles that
seek to express a viewpoint on something (or someone) need
fall back on the first person. Take the examples of good review-
writing considered back in Chapter 6: although they express
clear opinions on the strengths and weaknesses of what they are
critiquing, the reviewers manage to find ways of conveying their
views without having to rely on the clumsiness and unsubtlety
of first-person writing. One way of achieving this end is to adopt
a 'voice of authority': after all, if a reader is taking the time to
find out what you think about a book, film or performance,
it is fair to assume they consider you to be knowledgeable
and authoritative on the subject, and to have views worth

considering. The authoritative voice can take any of a number of forms, but it is at its most effective when expressed in a straight-talking style: *stating*, in no uncertain terms, what you consider to be good or bad about whatever it is you are reviewing. The following example, taken from a review of the stage musical *The Full Monty* by Michael Coveney, chief critic of leading West End website www.whatsonstage.com, breezily demonstrates how this can be achieved:

> ... although [writer Simon] Beaufoy's vividly unsubtle script touches on issues of impotency, suicide, incipient gay fulfil-ment, economic hardship and loss of self-esteem, the show is really a full-on blast of crude popular theatre in the great Northern tradition of Alan Bleasdale, Willy Russell and Alan Plater: those hob-nail boots are made for walking, and male strippers don't necessarily have to reveal glistening torsos and six-packs like the Chippendales. Women have 'knockers' and doorknobs are different.
>
> The great moment of a distracted chorus line in the job centre seduced into movement by Donna Sumner is intact, while the first signs of turning things round in a reces-sion are perpetrated when Kenny Doughty's ebullient Gaz – whose own spirit is fuelled by the young son he's in a custody dispute over – puts his arm round Craig Gazey's hilariously dejected Lomper; Lomper's broken into the factory to hang himself from an idle crane.
>
> (Michael Coveney, 'The Full Monty', www.whatsonstage.com, 26 February 2014)

Besides the fact that there is no technical reason Coveney *needs* to use the words 'I' or 'me', consider how much more vague and equivocal his review would have been if he had kept inserting phrases like 'in my opinion' or 'from my perspective', rather than having the confidence to praise (and criticize) the play directly. Phrases like 'vividly unsubtle script', 'great moment' and 'hilar-iously dejected' all implicitly express judgements about the merits of the show, yet the first person is nowhere in sight.

11. OTHER GENERAL ISSUES IN JOURNALISTIC WRITING

WRITING ACTIVELY AND VISUALLY, and recognizing when it is *not* necessary (or appropriate) to insert yourself into an article, may be key lessons for effective journalistic writing. But there are many more ways in which you can refine your written journalism to improve its flow and maximize its impact. Almost all of these come down to questions of *balance*: the balance between shorter and longer sentences, past and present tense, direct and indirect quotes and too much or too little punctuation. The following sections will examine some of the most frequent dilemmas journalists face as they grapple with the need to make their writing as accessible but evocative as possible.

Short versus Long Sentences: Striking the Right Balance

News stories, as we know, make a virtue of their (often extreme) brevity. To this end, it is widely accepted that they should not only be kept to a relatively short length, but that the individual sentences and paragraphs used to tell them ought to be tightly worded and economical. It is unusual to come across a tabloid story, for instance, much longer than 300 words – or with sentences numbering more than twenty-five. Moreover, each paragraph will tend to consist of a single sentence. In the case of features, reportage and essays, though, it is not only the length of the overall article that expands, but that of its component parts. While being assigned a longer-form piece to write does not give you a licence to ramble or overwrite, you usually have scope to experiment with a much wider *range* of sentence lengths (and structures) than the humble, hamstrung news reporter.

Some of the most vivid writing is that which employs a mix of both shorter and longer sentences. A colourful descriptive passage that begins with an initial sentence of generous length will often gain impact or emphasis from the addition of a pithy one immediately afterwards, and vice versa. As ever, determining when to tighten and loosen your wording is a question of journalistic judgement, and you will become better at judging the more you practice. Mark Twain memorably described the longer sentence as something a writer should only occasionally 'indulge' himself with – and on condition that, 'when he has done with it, it won't be a sea-serpent with half of its arches under the water', but rather 'a torch-light procession'. What follows is an example of one such 'torch-light procession'. It is extracted from the opening passage of a 'think piece' by Sholto Byrnes in left-leaning weekly news magazine the *New Statesman*. In it, Byrnes combines short and longer sentences to great effect, as he leads us through the key stages of Indonesia's recovery from its prolonged period under an authoritarian regime – an example he uses to illustrate the troubled democratization process that lies ahead for societies emerging from years of dictatorship during the Arab Spring:

> After weeks of riots, demonstrations and bloody counterat-tacks, the dictator at last stood down. His promised reforms were not enough. Eventually the armed forces, from whose ranks he had emerged and whose loyalty had shored up his regime for nearly 30 years, would no longer support him. Some feared that when elections were held, Islamists would take over. In the event, the first fair presidential vote did bring to power the leader of a Muslim organisation; but mod-eration prevailed. The country's citizens were too attached to their newly won freedom to allow anyone to restrict their rights again.

A decade on, corruption is rife, many of the dictator's past associates are big political players, and the former ruler was never brought to account for the human rights violations that took place on his watch. But change has come. The US president has hailed the country as a model for how Muslim-majority autocracies can become pluralist democracies.

(Sholto Byrnes, 'After the dictators', *New Statesman*,
12 September 2011)

We see a similar discipline at work in many of the most celebrated works of journalism. In *All the President's Men* (1974), the first half of Pulitzer Prize-winning reporters Carl Bernstein and Bob Woodward's epic account of how they broke the Watergate scandal – the revelation of a break-in at Democratic Party headquarters by men acting on behalf of Republican president Richard Nixon, which ultimately led to his resignation – the writers combine short and long sentences to memorable effect. What they produce is a compelling, page-turning narrative about one of the great political corruption exposés of modern times – an achievement all the more remarkable for their curious decision to write it in the third person, as if describing characters and events unknown to them personally.

'Drip-feeding' Information: The Art of Teasing the Reader

As well as boasting beautifully balanced sentences, the *New Statesman* example cited previously is also an example of the art of 'drip-feeding' the reader: giving them small morsels of information, a bit at a time, to entice them to read on to find out who, what or where *precisely* the journalist is writing about. In this case, it is not until the start of the paragraph following immediately on from the earlier extract that Byrnes reveals his hand, by spelling out the name of the country to which he is referring. It is a clever device which draws on the principles of the delayed drop for undeniable dramatic effect:

This is an outline of what happened when a long-serving dictator fell from power in 1998 – General Suharto of Indonesia. Can something similar happen in the Middle East and North Africa? For decades of their post-independence history, the countries of the Far East and south-east Asia were ruled by autocrats. One by one, however, nearly all the despots have fallen, or stepped down, or begun to open up their state's political sphere and relinquish power. In some countries, the change happened dramatically, as in Indonesia and in the Philippines' People Power Revolution of 1986, which saw off Ferdinand Marcos. In others, 'soft authoritarians' such as Singapore's Lee Kuan Yew and Malaysia's Mahathir Mohamad voluntarily terminated long periods in office. Democracy today may be limited, as it is in Singapore, shaky (Cambodia) or intermittent (Thailand). But principles of good governance, such as independence of the judiciary, took root so quickly in South Korea and Taiwan that both countries have tried and convicted democratically elected presidents.

(Sholto Byrnes, 'After the dictators', *New Statesman*, 12 September 2011)

Teasing readers in this way serves a function beyond the merely commercial: while advertisers are understandably drawn to publications that have mastered the art of hauling in readers slowly – and, crucially, holding their attention once they have it – articles also gain impact, in purely *narrative* terms, from the gradual unpacking of their twists and surprises. Here is another example, this time from *The Economist*. Although the strapline above the title ('America's Crumbling Infrastructure') gives the punchline away somewhat, the article itself reveals its hand more gradually:

THE Pulaski Skyway is a bridge of beauty, a lattice of steel held high above the river that separates Newark from Jersey City. It is also a bit rickety. Some of its struts have begun to resemble the pastry on a millefeuille. Its structure is described as 'basically intolerable' by the National Bridge Inventory. The thousands of motorists who cross it each day probably agree. With no money to pay for its maintenance, New Jersey re-classified the Pulaski as an entrance to a tunnel that maps suggest lies miles to its north, so that the Port Authority could be tapped for funds. For this, Chris Christie, the state's governor – who has had other troubles with bridges recently – finds his administration under investigation by the Securities and Exchange Commission and New York's District Attorney.

('Bridging the Gap', *The Economist*, London, June 2014)

Past versus Present Tense – and When to Use 'Which'

Illogical though it may sound, the convention with news stories is that they should always be told in the past tense. By definition, 'news' is about things that are 'new' – for which read, events and incidents that *have just* happened, *are going* to happen or *are* happening *now*. Why, then, should we worry about reporting them (grammatically speaking) as if they have happened in the *past*? One rationale for the convention of past-tense reporting is that reporters are meant to be in the business of writing about 'facts'. Using the past tense – 'said' rather than 'says', 'launched' instead of 'is launching', 'climbed' as opposed to 'will climb' – arguably lends journalistic writing a *definite* quality which marks it out from prediction or speculation. We can say that X has happened to Y because it *has*, and here are the quotes, statistics, photographs and/or videos to prove it. Describing something, as it happens, using the *present* tense does not, in theory, detract from its credibility or believability, and yet there is something inherently more concrete about an occurrence we can unequivocally say *has happened*. If nothing else, the passage of time since it occurred – weeks, days, hours, minutes or seconds – has given us the opportunity (however fleeting) to *define* it as 'a happening'.

This gives a *general* rationale for placing news in the past tense, but, perhaps surprisingly, there is actually a very *specific* one for doing so in relation to 'breaking' stories. By definition, journalists' knowledge of scenarios or events that are still unfolding changes continually, and it may become necessary for reports to be updated, clarified, amended or even corrected, at times, as details become clearer, are confirmed by officials and/or revised or contested by other parties. This is especially true in an online age, in which even 'print' journalists are expected to upload copy online as soon as possible after news of a story breaks – updating and embellishing it throughout the day, at the same time as they work on fuller, 'definitive' versions of the same story for that evening's or the next morning's newspaper.

The usefulness of the past tense in such cases is, as ever, best demonstrated by the use of a plausible example. Take, for instance, a road traffic accident in which two cars collide and several people are injured – a staple of local papers up and down the country and, when the crash is particularly spectacular or leads to tragic consequences, something in which even nationals might sometimes be interested. Let us suppose that one of the drivers involved in the collision (a married father-of-two) has been taken to intensive care with life-threatening injuries. A common approach to opening a story of this kind – and, sadly, a somewhat clichéd one – is wording along these lines:

A married father-of-two was fighting for his life this morning after his car overturned on the M1 in a collision with a delivery lorry.

Leaving aside the rather cynical emphasis on elements of the story journalists would judge especially newsworthy (the fact that this fictional driver happens to be married with two children and his car overturned), why is it preferable to write that he "*was* fighting for his life", rather than "*is*"? There are various answers to this question. Firstly, the fact that the motorist has life-threatening injuries and is in intensive care (details confirmed by the emergency services) means that, by definition, his condition could go either way. Put brutally, within the next few hours or days, it will either stabilize and improve – in which case, he will be transferred onto a normal hospital ward – or deteriorate further and he will die. In one sense, then, the reporter who writes that he '*was* fighting for his life' is doing little more than 'covering' him- or herself (and his/her news organization), by 'hedging bets' about which way the driver's condition will go. By stating that he 'was' in this condition at a more or less specific time of day, he/she is 'locating' this fact in time, in a way that any reporter who writes that someone *'is'* in that condition would not be. In so doing, he/she is guarding against the possibility that, at some point, the driver might take a turn for the worse and die – and that this could well happen before the journalist has been made aware of the fact, with the result that a story erroneously suggesting the man is still alive remains unaltered on the website or (even worse) on the printed page. Leaving aside the self-interested journalistic desire to avoid embarrassment, there are clear ethical issues at stake here. There is a very real prospect, for example, that anxious friends and relatives (in addition to periodically ringing the hospital) will be monitoring local news sites for updates on the injured man's plight, and that they would be cruelly misled by a news report which continues to state, in the *present* tense, that he is alive (albeit 'fighting for his life'). Using the past tense in such cases is, then, a question of both journalistic accuracy and sound ethical judgement. Although the problem of events overtaking the pace of news production was undoubtedly more acute in the pre-digital era – when, once the pages had been sent off, nothing could be done to intercept them before they appeared on news stands later the same day or the following morning – even today there is a short delay between news stories being written/edited and uploaded publicly on a website. If the 'holding copy' (the earliest version of a story) published on a site has it that the injured man is, rather than was, in a critical condition, then there is always a danger that, if he were to die, there would be a period of time during which an inaccurately positive account of his position remained publicly visible online. Of course, none of this detracts from the singular *advantage* online news reports have over print: namely, that as soon as an outdated detail or error is spotted it can be removed or corrected, in a way that is still impossible for 'hard copy' editions that have been bundled off to the printers.

While the past tense, then, is more commonly used in news-writing, this is less often the case in features, colour pieces, reportage and almost all other forms of journalistic prose. But why should the 'rules' governing longer-form journalism be any different? One reason for the conventional use of the present tense in features and other lengthier articles is that they tend to be concerned with getting 'under the skin' of a subject – an issue, debate, location and/or person – and, to that end, painting a more detailed and intimate portrait of it than we would expect to see in a simple news report. Though longer pieces do need to contain facts, rather than mere impressions or conjecture, they are concerned with giving readers a 'feel' for something: and if they can leave us with a tangible sense of how that something looks, sounds, tastes or smells, then so much the better. For instance, by using the present tense – informing us that an interviewee 'is wearing a buttoned-up suit, a stiff posture and a stern expression' – the journalist is *transporting* us into an encounter with someone who seems less than relaxed (or pleased to see the interviewer). If the journalist had used the word 'was' instead of 'is', the effect would arguably not have been so vivid: straightaway, the encounter becomes dislocated, or situated in the past, and there is a sense that we are having to rely on the journalist's fallible recollection of something that *did* happen, rather than *is* happening, to them. By contrast, the present tense approach has the effect of turning us into eye-witnesses: no longer are we reliant solely on the journalist describing something to us after the event (though in reality we still *are*). It is as if we are being empowered to see, hear and experience it for *ourselves*. As always, illustration helps. Though beginning with a clear statement of time and place – beaming us back to 'Wolverhampton, 5 April 1988', no less – the opening salvo of Caitlin Moran's award-winning memoir, *How to Be a Woman* (2011), is otherwise written in a breathless present tense which instantly transports us into her (very active) shoes, as she sprints away from bullies on her 'worst birthday ever' (the title of her first chapter):

WOLVERHAMPTON, 5 APRIL 1988
Here I am, on my 13th birthday. I am running. I'm running from The Yobs.

'Boy!'

'Gyppo!'

'Boy!'

I'm running from The Yobs in the playground by our house. It is a typical playground of Britain in the late eighties. There's no such thing as safety surfaces, ergonomic design or, indeed, slats on the benches. Everything's made of concrete, broken Corona pop bottles and weeds. As I run, I'm totally alone. I can feel the breath in my throat catching, like sick. I've seen nature documentaries like this before. I can see what's happening here. My role is, clearly, that of 'weak antelope, separated from the pack'. The Yobs are 'the lions'. I know this never really ends well for the antelope. Soon, my role will turn into a new one: that of 'lunch'.

'Yah pikey!'

I'm wearing Wellington boots, NHS glasses that make me look like Alan Bennett, and my dad's *Withnail*-style army coat. I do not, I admit, look very feminine. Diana, Princess of Wales is feminine. Kylie Minogue is feminine. I am … feminone. So I understand The Yobs' confusion. They do not look as if they have dabbled much in either a) the iconography of the counter-culture or b) the inspirational imagery of radical gender-benders. I imagine they were confused by both Annie Lennox and Boy George when they appeared on *Top of the Pops*.

(from How to be a Woman by Caitlin Moran, published by Ebury Press, 2012)

Direct Quotes versus Reported Speech

Journalism, as this book has repeatedly reiterated, is innately preoccupied with facts and opinions. On the one hand, journalists are (or should be) in the business of informing readers about things that are going on; on the other, they are involved in relaying to us what people and organizations with contrasting viewpoints and perspectives feel (for which read *say*) about those things. By definition, both these tasks require the use of quotations. It is one thing to write 'the Government is to launch a new crackdown on illegal drugs', but while this might seem a safe enough statement for us to believe (the scenario it paints being all-too familiar), far better to supply the 'proof' to back it up, by writing 'a new crackdown on illegal drugs was announced today by the Home Secretary'. By attributing the fact that a tough new anti-drugs initiative is to be launched to a specified individual with the authority and credibility to substantiate it (no less than the senior minister responsible for drugs policy), the reporter has authenticated his/her intro. Moreover, the conventions of news-writing demand that, by the third or fourth paragraph of the story, there should be a direct quote from the Home Secretary (or a spokesperson) further validating the intro angle and adding detail.

By definition, quotes are even more essential in the context of conveying individuals' and organizations' *opinions*. Many of the strongest news stories, and feature topics, are concerned with controversial or contentious issues and debates about which (whatever the objective 'facts') there may be any number of legitimate viewpoints. For good reason is it often said that nothing beats a good 'row' in journalism. In the interests of journalistic balance – but also of conveying the most dramatic, and therefore commercially appealing, story – it is incumbent on journalists to choose the most divergent, forcefully argued and well-articulated opinions to illustrate the level of disagreement between the opposing parties. A story opening with the claim 'residents and local businesses have condemned plans for a new bypass around Smalltown' must swiftly follow up this sentence with quotes from both groups, in order for readers to have the confidence that the paraphrased views expressed in the intro accurately reflect what opponents of the road are saying. Furthermore, in due course they will also need to include a 'right to reply' from the local authority and/or developers behind the proposed scheme, again in both the interests of balance and (from a narrative point of view) *demonstrating* the extent of disagreement between the two sides.

The need for quotations to be included in articles, then, is self-evident. But how should journalists go about deciding when and where to use *direct quotes*, as opposed to *reported speech*? Partly, as ever, this is a question of balance: speech marks act as handy 'signposts' as readers' eyes scan articles for evidence to *back up* facts/claims asserted by the writer, while, conversely, long strings of direct quotes can look just as unsightly as dense passages of reported ones. Both extremes also have the effect of requiring the *reader* to do too much of the *journalist's* work – by wading through lengthy quotations to sift out the most salient and/or interesting comments, or taking on trust the accuracy of the writer's interpretation (and paraphrasing) of others' opinions. There is something particularly lazy-looking about long, uninterrupted runs of direct quotations: if nothing else, journalists who rely too heavily on them give the impression that they are using other people's words to write their articles *for* them, rather than (as they should be) sifting out only the strongest quotes and interspersing these with their own impressions and observations, and those of relevant third parties.

A handy rule of thumb to help you decide when to use a direct quote in preference to relaying someone's comments in your own words is this: ask yourself which of the quotes you have in your notebook convey their views or arguments in clearer, more succinct and authentic language than you could possibly come up with yourself? Sometimes a direct quote is undeniably the best option. For example, if the speaker used slang, colloquialisms or expletives to express an angry opinion about something or someone – or summed up their feelings in an especially punchy or emotive sound-bite – direct quotes will tend to 'choose themselves' (notwithstanding your editor's likely aversion to too many swear words!) But the individuals you interview for articles are only human – and they almost always are individuals, in the end, as even quoting the collective or corporate viewpoints of organizations will require you to interview press officers or PRs authorized to speak on their behalf. As imperfect human beings, these interviewees do not always express what they are *trying* to say as eloquently they might. It is on these occasions, above all, that there is a clear role for reported speech. Journalists, after all, make their livings out of phrasing things, so it will often be the case that you *can* put across a thought or idea much more effectively – not to say concisely – in your own words, than by quoting the proverbial horse's mouth verbatim. But, whichever option you choose, be mindful of this advice: in choosing between direct quotes and reported speech to make a particular point, you do need to stick with one or the other. All too often one reads a news story or feature in which the journalist has summed up an interviewee's view or argument, only to then replicate this information immediately afterwards with a direct quote that says more or less exactly the same thing. This returns us to some of the most basic rules of journalistic writing: the need to write concisely, avoid repetition and observe the maxim that is less is often more. If something is better said in your own words, have the confidence to follow that through. If not, quote the speaker directly and have done with it.

The need to distinguish between quotes that are best conveyed exactly as spoken and those that can be summed up more effectively by you, or even left out of an article entirely, can prove especially problematic when the interviewee is well known, rich and powerful and/or used to dictating the terms on which interviews are conducted, and the words attributed to them. But, despite what they think, even famous interviewees are not always the most lucid speakers, and it may well be that you can hit the nail on the head more succinctly and precisely than they can. Try not to be intimidated by their status or celebrity: if you can sum up the essence of what they are saying more elegantly in your own words than verbatim quotes, then go with your instincts and do just that. Conversely, on the more frequent occasions when you find yourself interviewing members of the public – normally people with no prior experience of speaking to the media – you will often find that they stumble over words, or punctuate their sentences with 'ums' and 'ahs'. While you should always strive for authenticity in your quotes, it is accepted practice for journalists to 'tidy them up' to some extent – by, for example, editing out extended repetitions or tautologies. Again, the best course is often to dispense with some of the direct quotes, and 'sum up' the important points the person is trying to make in your own, more carefully chosen, words. In short, let your journalistic judgement determine if something is better expressed as originally spoken or as paraphrased or summarized by you.

None of this is to deny that, at times, it is best to let interviewees speak for themselves. The following extract is an example of when a particularly garrulous and amusing personality all-but 'takes over' their interview – in so doing, enlivening and animating it in a way that any amount of colourful third-person reporting would struggle to equal. In a feature (of sorts) for www.express.co.uk, journalist Kirsty McCormack is wise enough to do little more than *prompt* her interviewee, the 'motormouth' actor Brendan O'Carroll, before leaving him to speak unimpeded for long stretches about his famous alter ego, Irish matriarch Mrs Brown, and the curious nature of the repertory company he takes with him on tour – all of whom are family members:

'We're not the Waltons,' he laughed. 'We have our ups and downs but actually it's less difficult than what it would be if we weren't working together because all families have set to's with each other and they walk away and go home and might not talk again for two or three weeks so it simmers.

'But what happens with us is that at 8 o'clock every night we have to go onstage and be a family, so by the time the show is over and you come off, you look at each other and go "this is stupid".

He continued: 'I'm sure it has one or two downfalls, but I haven't found any yet! I've done stand-up for many, many years and stand-up sounds like a great gig, but it's a very lonely gig. It doesn't matter how many people are at the show, when you close your hotel door, it's just you, a microphone and a suit cover in the room and it's very lonely.

'But I get to tour with my son, daughter, my son-in-law, my daughter-in-law and my four grandsons, and every morning at half-past eight, no matter where we are, I get a knock on the door saying: "Granddad, cup of tea!"'

(Kirsty McCormack, 'Exclusive: Why Mrs Brown is as Feisty as Ever in D'Movie', *Daily Express*, 24 June 2014)

Even when interviewees do prove adept at speaking for themselves, however, it is important not to give them *too* free a rein – however entertaining they might be to just sit back and 'listen to'. As a journalist, it is vital to ensure you are 'controlling' the interview, which means directing the flow of the conversation itself – challenging evasions and steering interviewees away from deviations – but also assessing the value of what comes out of their mouths after the event, and using this assessment to guide the way in which you frame your article 'on the page'. If interview pieces become too dominated by the voice of the interviewee, the interviewer is all-but drowned out, and (as with weak Q&As) it is hard to be certain how effective his/her journalism has been. Moreover, interviews that resemble little more than long strings of verbatim quotes can produce lazy, dry and unengaging copy, as the journalists have effectively abdicated their roles as editors and observers by allowing their subjects to ramble on, unimpeded, determining their own agendas and (like as not) straying into humdrum, less newsworthy, areas – sometimes as a deliberate distraction from more sensitive topics about which they would rather not be questioned. Remember that, in the first instance, you should only ever interview someone who has something interesting and/or informative to tell you (and your audience). Think of your interviewee as a trapped genie you are releasing, for a short time only, in the hope they will reveal their secrets. The trick is to make sure you know when to put them back in the bottle.

The following extract with another vocal interviewee, the former Sex Pistols singer John Lydon, is an object lesson in this approach. In it, journalist Andrew Perry skilfully alternates between direct and indirect quotes to relay Lydon's transatlantic perspective on Britain as he returns home for a reunion of his more recent band, Public Image Limited. As with all good interviewees, Perry is not afraid to challenge his subject – for example, confronting him with the apparent hypocrisy of his more mainstream money-making ventures – or translate less quotable comments into his terms:

Now 53, he unashamedly sports the bright-orange, spiky

hair of his youth, and revels in firing off withering asides about cultural developments at home, from Gordon Ramsay ('he only got famous by stealing my Anglo-Saxon vocabulary'), and Harry Redknapp ('a dodgy car salesman'), to the BNP.

'If ever anybody got the Sex Pistols wrong, it was that lot,' he says, referring to the fascist skinheads, who appropriated the Pistols' sound in the late 1970s. 'Britain's an island, it's always had a constant ebb and flow of immigration, it makes it a better place. And there's not a BNP hooligan in existence that can do without his curry on a Saturday night, right?' He laughs, scornfully. 'There's no brain challenge with these morons.'

Lydon's own dalliances in mainstream culture have, however, earnt him equally scathing criticism: does the original punk rocker have any business starring in a TV advert for Country Life butter? He impatiently argues that such projects have enabled him to finance his PiL reunion.

(Andrew Perry, 'John Lydon interview', www.telegraph.co.uk, 25 November 2009)

Besides authenticating the factual basis of an article – in essence, acting as the 'evidence' that backs up the writer's assertions, in much the same way as they are used in essays – quotes can serve other important journalistic functions, too. Chief among these is their use as a story-telling device in themselves. Consider this extract from Martha Gellhorn's seminal *Justice at Night*, in which the fearless reporter hands over the page to what is effectively a transcript of hers and her colleagues' unsettling exchange with a truck-driver who pulls over to offer them a lift in the wilds of Mississippi on the condition that they accompany him to the 'lynching' of a black teenager wrongly accused of raping an ageing white widow. The authenticity of this encounter rests, in large part, on Gellhorn's uncompromising decision to quote the driver's brutally racist language uncensored – an approach many journalists and publications might balk at today:

I said timidly, 'Who's getting lynched?'

'Some goddam nigger, name of Hyacinth as I recollect.'

'What did he do?'

'He got after a white woman.' I began to think with doubt and disgust of this explanation. So I asked who the woman was.

'Some widow woman, owns land down towards Natchez.'

'How old is she?' Joe asked. Joe was in doubt, too. 'Christ, she's so old she ought to of died. She's about forty or fifty.'

'And the boy?'

'You mean that nigger Hyacinth?'

I said yes, and was told that Hyacinth was about nineteen, though you couldn't always tell with niggers; sometimes they looked older than they were and sometimes younger.

'What happened?' Joe said. 'How do you know she got raped?'

'She says so,' the driver said. 'She's been screaming off her head about it ever since this afternoon. She run down to the next plantation and screamed and said hang that man; and she said it was Hyacinth. She ought to of knowed him anyhow; he was working for her some-time back.'

'How do you mean; was he a servant?'

'No,' the driver said, 'he was working on her land, on shares. Most of her croppers moved off by now; she don't give them any keep and they can't make the crop if they don't get nothing to eat all winter. She sure is cruel hard on niggers, that woman; she's got a bad name for being a mean one.'

'Well,' Joe said, very gently, 'it doesn't look likely to me that a boy of nineteen would go after a woman of forty or fifty. Unless she's very beautiful of course.'

'Beautiful,' the man with the bottle said, 'Jees, you ought to see her. They could stick her out in a field and she'd scare the crows to death.'

(Martha Gellhorn, 'Justice at Night', *The Spectator*, 20 August 1936)

Gellhorn might just as easily have relayed this encounter in her own words, as she does to great effect elsewhere. On this occasion, though, she purposely chooses to take a back-seat (in a metaphorical, as well as literal, sense) – handing the wheel over to the bottle-swigging stranger, whose implausible account of an alleged crime, and the violent punishment awaiting its supposed perpetrator, drives the narrative over the space of the following page. In this case, then, her use of verbatim dialogue serves two purposes: firstly to *prove* this story (in all its implausibility) was reported to her as written, and secondly to replace the 'journalist-narrator' with the voices of the *participants* in this unfolding horror show (including Gellhorn herself). In so doing, she is showing, rather than telling, us what happened – and foreshadowing, balefully, what is *about to happen*. Even using the past tense, rather than the present, she has transported us right into the very heart of the encounter, as if we were rocking along in that back-seat beside her.

A Brief Warning about Clichés (and Puns)

It is generally agreed that clichés and puns are best avoided in journalism almost all of the time. In his classic 'how-to' (or, perhaps, 'how-not-to') guide to journalistic English, the late *Daily Mail* columnist, novelist and screen-writer Keith Waterhouse listed no fewer than ten reasons why puns should be avoided – however tempting it might be to use them. Chief among these were that they are out-of-date or anachronistic, in poor taste (for instance, the infamous *Daily Mirror* headline 'Blow me' about a hurricane that killed numerous people), obscure, or simply too obvious (the reports about a well-known comedian whose admission into hospital was expected to leave his nurses 'in stitches'). But rules are made to be broken (to coin a cliché), and there will certainly be occasions when using an otherwise hackneyed turn of phrase 'feels' apposite, if not irresistible. Even then, it is wise to approach it with caution. Another widely accepted ground-rule of written journalism is that, even where their use is appropriate, puns, alliteration and clichés should generally be left to sub-editors. It is no coincidence that the most celebrated examples of the form – for example, *The Sun's* 'Zip me up before you go go', over a story about former Wham! singer

George Michael being arrested for 'cottaging' in a gentlemen's public toilet – are drawn not from the body text of articles, but from their headlines. Nonetheless, as long as you use wordplay selectively, there are likely to be (very rare) occasions when such conceits are justified. One might imagine, for instance, a story about a dispute between rival orchestras – or, indeed, members of the same orchestra – which merits the use of a term like 'discord' or 'disharmony' to describe the row or rift. A nuanced, well-judged device of this kind arguably adds a neat touch which would not have worked nearly as well (if at all) had the argument described been between, say, two footballers or political parties.

Humour – When and How to Use it

On the whole, journalism is in the business of being direct and informative. To this end, there is little room for irony or sarcasm in most forms of journalistic writing, and as each is notoriously difficult to judge and apply effectively, in any case, they are generally best avoided. Moreover, as with puns and clichés, questions of taste should intervene to tell you when it is absolutely *not* suitable to be cracking jokes (it is clearly off-limits in articles about death and destruction, bereavement, war, famine, poverty or any other form of human tragedy). That said, colour writing, comment pieces and reviews, in particular, can benefit greatly from subtle flashes of humour. Indeed, much of the writing quoted up to this point – from the outlandish scenarios described in Wolfe's *Electric Kool Aid Acid Test* to the gently mocking understatement of Ronson's *Big Brother* piece to the endearingly self-deprecating opening to Moran's *How to be a Woman* – exhibit a keen sense of pathos and the absurd.

It is these sorts of playful journalistic humour – a world away from the scabrous satire of *Punch* or even *Private Eye*, which is best left to 'professional' humourists and political sketchwriters – that, used in small doses, can be useful tools in the feature-writer's, essayist's or even reporter's armoury. Take this audacious opening to an otherwise (more or less) straight news backgrounder by former *Independent on Sunday* foreign editor

David Randall. It focuses on the marriage break-up of media tycoon Rupert Murdoch and his wife, Wendi Deng. Randall's knowingly wry, 'nudge-nudge' dropped intro is entirely framed around a reference to the still-ongoing saga over the use of 'phone-hacking' by journalists at Murdoch's *News of the World* to tap into the private voicemail messages of celebrities, politicians and members of the public in search of stories. By referring to a long-running scandal he is confident will be familiar to most, or all, of his readers, he is using a crafty conceit to make what might have been a humdrum account of Murdoch's already widely publicized marital difficulties into a classic Sunday think-piece that is very much his own:

> If only someone could invent a way of eavesdropping on Rupert Murdoch's voicemail messages, or hacking into Wendi Deng's emails, or even finding a public official who was happy to be bribed. Then the world might learn just what it is that caused the 82-year-old billionaire to file for divorce from his formidable 44-year-old wife.

(David Randall, 'Rupert Murdoch and Wendi Deng hire his'n'hers legal teams', www.independent.co.uk, 15 June 2013)

'Don't Use Semi-colons!' The Perils of the Extended Pause

If there is one punctuation mark, above all others, that it is wise for journalists to avoid, it is the semi-colon. While commas and full-stops are crucial building-blocks of effective sentences/paragraphs and there is no avoiding the use of quotation marks to denote direct speech, or apostrophes to show possession, it is rare for writers to *need* to use semi-colons – and rarer still for writers to use them correctly.

For the uninitiated, the semi-colon – in crude terms, a cross between a comma and a colon – has two principal grammatical functions. These are, firstly, to denote a pause that is longer than that created by a comma, but shorter than one indicated by a colon or full-stop; and (as used here) to connect two or more related thoughts or ideas in a single sentence. These two functions tend to be inextricably linked: the act of separating related thoughts or ideas within the confines of one sentence *requires* the presence of punctuation marks to denote the separations. Most commonly, semi-colons will be used to 'list' two or more items within a sentence when each of those items is a *phrase* rather than a word. Whereas a simple list of clothing items, for example, might be separated by commas (as in 'shirts, coats, trousers and socks'), a more detailed version of the same might justify, or require, semi-colons (e.g. 'cream-coloured shirts with braces; long-tailed, double-breasted coats; flared trousers with pockets on either side; and red socks with diamond patterns'). A mini master-class on how to deploy the semi-colon in this way is offered by the extract from Dickens' 'Crime and Education' quoted on p.97.

Suffice it to say, most journalists (in fact, most *writers*) struggle with such nuanced distinctions. And, in truth, the wider conventions of journalistic writing seldom render semi-colons either desirable or necessary. Even longer-form articles will generally avoid the need for journalists to list long trains of complex items, or ideas, in the space of a single sentence, while the separation of two distinct parts of a sentence can normally be achieved by using a dash or colon (as here): the words before it being used to 'set up' a point to which the writer is building, and those after it to *emphasize* that point or deliver a surprise punchline. As a result, a tip (if not command) oft-repeated by journalism trainers and sub-editors in newsrooms up and down the land is the following: semi-colons are best avoided!

House Style

No examination of the craft of journalistic writing would be complete without brief mention of the concept of 'house style'. Although the primary engine of prose accuracy is the 'rule-book' of English grammar (spelling and punctuation), most publications expect their journalists to respect additional conventions when committing particular terms or items to the page. A long-standing tradition in written journalism is for publishers to issue their writers with copies of their own 'house style guides': lengthy, occasionally exhaustive, A–Z lists of their preferred wording for everything from dates to weights and measures to job titles. They will also tend to specify when their journalists should (and should not) use initial capitals, as opposed to lower-case letters; when numbers should be expressed in words, rather than figures; and whether percentages should be written in the style 'percent', 'per cent' or '%'.

The aim of such style guides is to achieve a sense of consistency, uniformity and (to borrow a contemporary buzz-phrase) 'brand identity' that marks one publication/publisher out from another, while simultaneously adhering to certain industry-wide conventions that have emerged over time. To take one example, there is a broad consensus among British newspapers (both local and national) that numbers should be written out in full from one to nine, but printed as 10, 11, etc. once they reach double figures. That said, even here there are some inconsistencies, with certain titles writing out the word 'ten' and only switching to figures from eleven onwards. By the same token, in British newspapers dates are commonly written in the following style – 'September 11', rather than '11/9' or '9/11' – with the exception of a handful of titles (notably the *Independent* and *Independent on Sunday*) that prefer to reverse this, as in '11 September'. Similarly, though there has been a tendency over time to reduce the number of occasions on which journalists use initial capital letters, in general they are always used for Christian and surnames and other so-called *proper nouns* – defined by the Oxford English Dictionary as the 'name used for an individual person, place, or organization'. In this vein, newspapers and magazines tend to use initial caps more rather than less often, with, for example, the holders of certain unique job titles, or those occupying particular honorary or inherited positions, also being 'capped up' when they are referred to in writing. Hence, the Queen, the Prime Minister, the Foreign Secretary, the Pope, the Archbishop of Canterbury (to cite a handful) will all be capitalized on the page, in most cases – with the caveat that, if writers are referring to holders of such positions in the *plural*, they will tend to revert to lower-case initials (i.e. queens, prime ministers, foreign secretaries, popes, arch-bishops of Canterbury). However, even in the context of proper noun usage there are high-profile exceptions: in recent years, the *Guardian* and *Observer* have increasingly shied away from using initial caps to an almost obsessive extent, with even the names of certain institutions, such as the House of Commons or the Church of England, routinely appearing with lower- rather than upper-case initials.

The stipulations of house style might seem a little pedantic, but consider this: how professional would a publication appear if some of its articles used one style, and the rest another; let alone if a mix of styles appeared in the same piece of writing? Indeed, in the digital age, with more people writing and publishing jour-nalism (of one order or other) than ever before, the concept of house style has lately been enjoying something of a renaissance. In fact, there is so much interest in it that many mainstream newspapers and magazines make their house style guides freely available online. The *Telegraph* newspapers, *The Guardian*, *The Observer* and *The Economist* are just three of Britain's national papers to publish their guides on a free-for-all basis. Of these, the latter opens with perhaps the most salutary general advice – quoting 'six elementary rules' set out by Orwell in his classic 1946 'plain English' manifesto, *Politics and the English Language*. We have rehearsed most of these at various points in this book, but it seems apt to close our chapters on writing technique with the great writer's short summation, as it has arguably never been bettered:

1. Never use a metaphor, simile or other figure of speech which you are used to seeing in print.
2. Never use a long word where a short one will do (see Short words).
3. If it is possible to cut out a word, always cut it out (see Unnecessary words).
4. Never use the passive where you can use the active.
5. Never use a foreign phrase, a scientific word or a jargon word if you can think of an everyday English equivalent.

6. Break any of these rules sooner than say anything out-right barbarous (see Iconoclasm).

(George Orwell, 'Politics and the English Language', *Horizon*,
April 1946)

In any style guide worth the name, all these maxims appear, in one form or other, to this day.

12. THE EDITING PROCESS

No ASPECT OF JOURNALISTIC writing is more time-consuming than editing. As any experienced practitioner will tell you, being asked to deliver an extra 200, 500 or even 1,000 words of copy when a 'hole' suddenly opens up on the page can be a positive pleasure. All at once you are free to embellish details and dig out quotes previously consigned to the cutting-room floor (in other words, your notebook). Indeed, being called on to expand a story or feature can often *improve* it, by liberating your writing from the confines of an artificially tight space which was only ever thus because the page it appeared on was worth more to the paper's proprietors when the bulk of it was filled by a paid-for advertisement, as opposed to editorial. But while it may be easy enough to produce *more* words (should the need arise), it can be far, far harder to write *fewer*. Editing is tough. It requires you to discard as much of your research as you end up display-ing; to spend an age cutting for one editor what another might have welcomed, or invited. Put simply: editing is where the hard work really begins ...

Time and Space: Editing to Length/Word Count

Editing exists because there simply isn't enough space (or time) to go round. In written journalism, the principal enemy is space: articles are laid out on the page, or online, and you are only ever given so much room in which to write them. Staff reporters and writers will generally be ordered at the outset to deliver stories and features to a specific word count that is dictated as much by financial considerations – whether an advert can be sold and, if so, how large an ad – as any objective assessment of its newsworthiness. Freelancers, meanwhile, are in most cases commissioned for a set number of words – and their fees will often directly correlate with the word count (or 'lineage') they are asked to produce. It is not uncommon, however, for further cuts to be demanded if another ad is sold. More rarely, you might occasionally find yourself being asked to produce 'extra' words, should an existing ad be pulled. Still less often, a commissioning editor might have a change of heart and decide that an article he/she previously deemed worthy of relatively few words is deserving of a larger, or more prominent, slot. All these decisions – which, in a busy newsroom environment, can vary from one minute to the next – have real implications for the editing process.

Although writers invariably disagree with editors and sub-editors about how long – or short – an article should be, there is rarely scope for negotiation, and it is their job to deliver the required number of words to deadline. Failure to do so will result in a reprimand (at the very least), and staff journalists have been sacked for less serious misdemeanours than repeatedly failing to file to length and on time. For freelancers, overwriting, underwriting and tardiness can be equally fatal: earning a living as a self-employed writer requires you to follow orders to the letter, so the penalty for unreliability will, at the very least, be failure to secure future commissions. The ability to edit quickly and effectively is, then, a crucial journalistic skill.

Onerous though it frequently is, though, it is important to be clear that editing is not always driven solely by commercial considerations. Even in physical publications (newspapers, magazines, periodicals), which have finite paginations and clear costs attached to every additional page printed, there is often a good reason why a story or feature needs to be cut. In its purest sense, editing is about *improving* a piece of writing – cutting out the flab, or slack, and making what remains clearer and more precise. Consider, for example, an oft-used phrase like 'ran quickly'. Why is it necessary to include the adverb 'quickly'? Surely it is tautological to write that someone is running quickly: by its nature, running is an action *intended* to be fast, and most runners will certainly be moving faster than those merely walking. But hold on (one might argue): just because someone is running does not mean they are travelling at great speed. After all, some people are capable of running faster than others. Nonetheless, this example acts as an illustration of how routinely we use phrases that (both in speech and writing) might be clarified and improved through editing. One might easily think of other examples along similar lines: to say that someone has 'climbed the wall', for instance, is arguably an improvement on saying they 'climbed *up* the wall', while stating that they 'sat down on the chair' could easily be economized simply to 'sat on the chair'. Editing, then, is not always (or only) about cost, or even time: it is about honing and precision.

A more general tip for editing is to start out by combing your copy for any wasted words (a key element of Orwell's advice, cited on pp.201–2). Over time, this should become second nature, to such an extent that you will find yourself mentally subediting everything in the world around you – never mind utility bills, cereal packets, junk mail and all the other assorted written matter you encounter in everyday life. Why write 'prior to' when you could say 'before', for instance – or 'is set to' (a well-worn journalistic idiom) when you really mean 'will'? How much snappier, and more active, to describe how a car 'screeched', rather than 'came screeching', to 'a halt'. Just as shorter words should generally be used in preference to longer ones – 'but' rather than 'however', 'rise' instead of 'increase' etc. – single words can often be substituted for phrases, with no resultant loss of meaning.

The Nuances of Cutting (against the Clock) – Shaving versus 'Slash-and-burn'

So how should journalists attend to the task of cutting to length? Put simply, editing needs to be approached on a case-by-case basis: how difficult and time-consuming a job it is will depend on how many words need to be cut, and how swiftly. In most instances, you will find that the number of words you need to remove relates to the size of the commissioned article: the bigger the piece, the bigger the cut. If you have been asked to write a 3,000-word feature (a rarity these days), and have carried out the detailed background research such an article normally demands, you are likely to face having to cut words in the hundreds, if not thousands, rather than tens or dozens. If you find yourself hacking as many words as this out of what was meant to be a short news piece, you must have seriously over-researched (and over-written) in the first place. With practice, this scenario is unlikely to arise very often. Seriously over-length articles may well require fairly brutal cuts – a process that can be likened more to 'slash-and-burn' than the sort of pruning and tightening required to trim a 350-word story back to 300. On other occasions, it is usually safe to shave in small chunks, a bit at a time.

But, however imminent your deadline, and however many words you need to lose, you must always try to approach the editing process with care. When you are struggling to cut out hundreds of words against the clock, it is very easy to produce a finished result that sacrifices meaning and accuracy in the service of brevity and speed. If editing from the top (as most journalists do), you need to be mindful of the fact that whatever you cut from earlier paragraphs will have a 'trickledown effect'. For instance, if you remove the name of one of the article's key players from your intro – perhaps their job title will suffice as an identifier to begin with – you must remember to insert their full name when you do get round to mentioning them (replacing 'Mr Smith' with the name 'Stephen Smith' you cut from the earlier paragraph). To use a metaphor, think of your copy as a knitted garment: snag or tug a thread too hard and the whole thing is likely to start unravelling, from the top downwards.

Proofreading and Basic Sub-editing for Grammar, Spelling and Style

The final stage of the editing process is one which, in an ideal world, would probably be best performed by someone else entirely. So important is it, in fact, that if you are writing for a book publisher, this is normally what happens: a professional proofreader will be hired to go over the manuscript with a fine-toothed comb to check for errors of spelling, grammar or house style.

Traditionally, a similar role to this has been fulfilled in written journalism by sub-editors or copy-editors, with many newspapers and magazines even going so far as to employ senior subs – known as 'copy-tasters' – to give articles a final once-over before they are sent to the printers. In the online era, however, things have changed, and many publications have now all-but dispensed with staff subs, leaving this all-important proofreading stage to the writers themselves. Indeed, web-only papers and magazines – particularly 'digital-native' start-ups that have only recently begun publishing – commonly have no 'filter' between their writers and the public, leaving journalists responsible for writing their own headlines and captions, and vulnerable to having to take full responsibility for any errors that do creep in.

For today's multi-tasking, multimedia journalists, the final proofreading stage has, then, become even more laborious – and vital – than ever before. This is the point at which you read back over your copy just before filing it, to ensure that it contains all the facts and figures you mean it to, is nicely written and, crucially, still makes sense. The best advice to aid you in the process of effective proofreading is that you should take a good, long 'screen-break' before you even embark on the task. In the absence of another individual capable of bringing to your copy a genuinely 'fresh eye', it is incumbent on you to 'freshen your own up' as much as you can.

AFTERWORD

The only qualities essential for real success in journalism are rat-like cunning, a plausible manner, and a little literary ability.

(Nicholas Tomalin)

The difference between literature and journalism is that journalism is unreadable and literature is not read.

(Oscar Wilde)

Taken at face value, neither of these quotes cast journalism in a complimentary light. Tomalin (a journalist himself) at least credited his fellow 'hacks' with a modicum of 'literary ability'. By contrast, Wilde exhibited the same snobbery towards the supposed aesthetic limitations of journalistic writing that prompted Cyril Connolly to remark that, while 'literature is the art of writing something that will be read twice', the best journalism can aspire to is a form of prose whose meaning can be 'grasped at once'.

Yet, even if we accept these limitations, there is much to be said for a writing tradition that (at its best) informs, educates and entertains in equal measure – and succeeds in communicating complex ideas and opinions in a way that enlightens and engages. Of course, not all journalism achieves these lofty ends; much of it, in the rush, falls some way short. But when journalists manage to demystify jargon-laden management-speak, technobabble and 'officialese' in ways that accurately translate what they mean, without *dumbing down* those meanings, they have arguably done more than merely catching our eye and providing us with a fleeting diversion: they have performed a valuable public service. Moreover, while Connolly and Wilde might have viewed journalistic writing as ephemeral and of little or no literary merit, in the classical sense, many of the extracts reproduced in this book – particularly those drawn from longer works – demonstrate that, at its best, written journalism can be every bit as evocative, exciting, moving and powerful as the most accomplished novels. In Bly's *Ten Days in a Mad-House*, Gellhorn's *Justice at Night*, Capote's *In Cold Blood* and Thompson's *Hell's Angels*, all human life is on show, in its glory and its grimness, and seldom is it rendered in anything less than the most vivid and penetrating prose.

Another enduring facet of journalism – in many ways, its unique selling-point – is the sheer *variety* of forms in which it can appear. Leaving aside its many *mediums* (television, radio, film, etc.), in writing alone it is published in a bewildering array of guises – from tweets and ticker tape-style news feeds beamed to people's smartphones to day-to-day newspaper stories, reviews and features to book-length reportage, travelogues, histories and biographies. And so preoccupied have some journalists been at times with the importance of clear and vivid writing – as concerned as Connolly or Wilde ever were – that they have put their names to books and articles about the 'art' of journalistic prose that have become classics in their own right. Orwell, Evans, Waterhouse, Wells – all are authors of oft-cited guides to English usage that have outsold, and out-published, any number of treatises like Connolly's priggish, long out-of-print *Enemies of Promise*.

This is not to say that Connolly's criticisms should be dismissed out of hand. For all its virtues, written journalism can be prone to many (if not all) of the vices and limitations he identifies. The sheer speed with which so much journalistic output is (necessarily) generated militates against polish and elegance, and limits the artistry we can realistically expect of it. And it is often said that it is possible to be an excellent news reporter without being much of a 'writer'. Writing itself is, after all, only one stage of the reporting process, and the ability to spot a news-worthy angle and the tenacity to pursue it until you have the story are, in the end, equally (if not more) important. It is not just the quality of a journalist's prose that we need to evaluate, but its *substance*: in essence, what he or she is writing about. Set in this context, the journalist's role as eyewitness, as watchdog, as chronicler, as opinion-former is what matters most. But if these facets can be displayed 'on the page' with eloquence and insight, then so much the better. It was Phillip Graham, erstwhile president and publisher of the *Washington Post*, who once memorably described journalism as 'the first rough draft of history', and perhaps this is how we should view most workaday journalistic writing – not as fully formed and final, but as rough sketches or (interrupted) works in progress. Indeed, even the best of the writing considered here – the features, reportage and essays about topics of particular concern at particular points in time – are *drafts*, in the sense that they were conceived and executed in response to great issues and debates of their day. Yet if all prose writers (novelists and playwrights included) could produce drafts as textured and searching as these, our culture might well be a good deal more literary – and literate – than it is today.

So all that remains is for us to answer the million-dollar question: how does one go about 'becoming' a prose journalist? Assuming you have no family connections in what is still loosely considered 'the industry' (as in most professions, nepotism and old school tie networks can get you a long way), it's invariably a case of starting at the bottom. And this is where the options have become more varied and uncertain than they were even ten or fifteen years ago. While most novices still tend to start out (post-training) in an entry-level job – a local weekly paper, trade magazine, e-zine, or news website – a growing number are breaking into the sector, however slowly, as entrepreneurial 'self-starters', through blogging, online social media, or by setting up their own DIY digital publications for niche audiences.

How, then, did we get to where we are – and what avenues are there (besides the dreaded unpaid 'internship') for those seeking a 'proper' journalistic training? Until recently, aspiring prose journalists faced a clear choice: they opted to write for either newspapers (in print and, latterly, online) or magazines/periodicals. In the good old days it was possible to obtain a job as a cub reporter on a local paper straight from school or college. While your starting salary would have been meagre (little has changed there), you would have been trained up on the job at no personal cost. To this end, 1951 saw the formation of the National Council for the Training of Journalists (NCTJ), an industry-led body which set up training centres to which editors could send their junior staff on block release. Here they would be schooled not only in the essentials of news-gathering and writing, but many of the other core skills trainees are still examined on to this day – from shorthand to media law and knowledge of public affairs (the workings of local and central government). But for those keen to break into longer-form journalism – writing for magazines or newspaper features sections and supplements – job (and training) opportunities were rarer. In the absence of the 'connections' needed to leapfrog you into one of the few, hallowed, staff posts available, it was a question of pursuing freelance opportunities, by doggedly pitching ideas for individual articles to commissioning editors 'from outside'. The hope was that, over time, you might build up a sufficiently impressive portfolio of published writing to catch the eye of other editors without the need to pitch for every assignment – perhaps one day even landing one of those few precious jobs.

As the old French saying goes, 'the more things change, the more they stay the same'. Having initially been prepared to train up the next generation of reporters itself, by the 1970s the newspaper industry had wised up to the fact that journalism had become such a popular career path it could now expect wannabe reporters to foot the bill themselves. It was around this time that many of today's three-month 'fast-track' training courses were set up by further education and technical colleges – normally with the NCTJ's stamp of approval – and even universities began to get in on the act by offering longer, more immersive and substantial, courses for graduates. City University in the heart of London – a stone's throw from the old Fleet Street – and the University of Wales, Cardiff, were the pioneers, and since then numerous nine-month and year-long diplomas and MAs have sprung up, with the universities of Sheffield, Kingston, Glasgow Caledonian, Strathclyde, Brunel, Kent, and Liverpool John Moores among the most respected providers of vocational journalism degrees today. More recently, some of these centres – City, Cardiff, and Kingston among them – have begun offering professional preparation magazine courses as well as newspaper ones. The most successful (i.e. the courses with the best track records for steering graduates into paid work at the end) tend to be those accredited by either the NCTJ or the trade body representing magazine publishers: the Periodical Training Council (PTC).

But, for all their proven strengths, the best university courses do not come cheap. Even a fast-track NCTJ diploma is liable to set you back anything between £1,000 and £2,000, while a year-long MA at a respected university will cost at least £7,000, and perhaps twice as much. Funding your training, then, can present at least as big a challenge for those from less comfortable backgrounds as landing a place on one of these famously competitive courses in the first place. Thankfully, though, there have been some recent efforts made to address the funding gap for those least able to call on the support of family or friends. Traditionally, candidates who secure places on journalism training courses have been eligible to apply for government-backed career development loans (CDLs) from one of the commercial banks involved in the scheme (Barclays and the Co-operative are among these). While CDLs incur interest, this tends to be at a much lower rate than one would expect from a normal commercial loan. And, if you do not immediately find work at the end of your course, the government will pay the interest for a period of months afterwards, to cushion you as you hunt for jobs. More recently, universities have begun offering various kinds of bursaries and scholarships designed to attract journalism students from a wider range of backgrounds – for example: ethnic minorities, postcode areas with high levels of social deprivation, and families in which no one has previously been through higher education. Even some local authorities still offer means-tested discretionary grants to those from poorer backgrounds to cover their course fees (if not living costs). Finally, the NCTJ has lately launched its own Journalism Diversity Fund. Initially targeted at promising young black and Asian journalists (it was founded, at least in part, in response to a startling survey showing how few of them made it into regional or national newsrooms), its remit has since widened to cover a variety of other 'minorities' – from first-generation university students to mature applicants struggling to balance their studies with family commitments and/or work.

For the most gifted and/or persistent, meanwhile, there remain a handful of 'direct-entry' places available each year on internal training programmes run by media organizations themselves. Graduate schemes of this kind are, or have periodically been, offered by Trinity Mirror (publisher of the *Daily Mirror*, *Sunday Mirror* and *Daily Record*, among other titles), *The Guardian*, the *Daily Telegraph*, the *Daily Mail*, *The Sun* and the BBC – not to mention major national and international news agencies, including Reuters, the Associated Press (AP) and the Press Association (PA). Not only are these traineeships and/or paid internships usually fully funded (often at the level of what many local reporters would consider handsome salaries), but their other great virtue is that they provide on-the-job training that, invariably, leads to full-time staff positions on household-name national titles.

As we advance through the second decade of the twenty-first century, then, the routes into journalism are more numerous and, potentially, accessible than they have been for decades. Though the days of 'on-the-job' training may be long gone, a belated recognition of the over-dominance of white, middle-class, highly educated young reporters and writers in our newsrooms has shocked colleges, universities and, to some extent, the industry itself into widening the net from which they select the prose journalists of tomorrow. Long may this last.

BIBLIOGRAPHY

Beckett, Andy, *When the Lights Went Out* (Faber and Faber, 2009)

Bernstein, Carl and Woodward, Bob, *All the President's Men* (Simon & Schuster, 1974)

Bly, Nellie, *Ten Days in a Mad-House* (Ian L. Munro, 1887)

Capote, Truman, *In Cold Blood* (Random House, 1966)

Connolly, Cyril, *Enemies of Promise* (Routledge and Kegan Paul, 1938)

Evans, Harold and Crawford, Gillan, *Essential English for Journalists, Editors and Writers*, first published as *Newsman's English* (William Heinemann, 1972)

Freedland, Jonathan, *Bring Home the Revolution: The Case for a British Republic* (Fourth Estate, 1998)

Hadley, Louisa, *Responding to Margaret Thatcher's Death* (Palgrave Macmillan, 2014)

Harris, John, *The Last Party* (Fourth Estate, 2003)

Hemingway, Ernest, *In our Time* (Boni & Liveright, 1925)

Hersh, Seymour, *My Lai 4: A Report on the Massacre and its Aftermath* (Random House, 1970)

Moran, Caitlin, *How to be a Woman* (Ebury Press, 2011)

Moreton, Cole, *Hungry for Home* (Viking, 2000)

Orwell, George, *Down and Out in Paris and London* (Victor Gollancz, 1933)

Orwell, George, 'England Your England' in *The Lion and the Unicorn* (Secker and Warburg, 1941)

Pilger, John (ed.), *Tell Me No Lies: Investigative Journalism and its Triumphs* (Cape, 2004)

Riis, Jacob, *How the Other Half Live* (Charles Schoner & Sons, 1890)

Sergeant, John, *Give Me Ten Seconds* (Macmillan, 2001)

Smith, Jon and Joanne Butcher, *Essential Reporting: The NCTJ Guide for Trainee Journalists* (Sage, 2007)

Thompson, Hunter S., *Hell's Angels: A Strange and Terrible Saga* (Ballantine Books, 1966)

Waterhouse, Keith, *Waterhouse on Newspaper Style* (Revel Barker, 1989)

Wells, H.G., 'The Writing of Essays' (1897) in *Certain Personal Matters* (T. Fisher Unwin, 1901)

Wilde, Oscar, 'The Critic as Artist' in *Intentions and Other Writings* (Doubleday, 1891)

Wolfe, Tom, *The Electric Kool Aid Acid Test* (Farrar Straus Giroux, 1968)

INDEX OF NAMES

Ahmed, Samira 133

Amis, Martin 10, 70

Anderson, Clive 119

Anthony, Andrew 60

Arnold, Matthew 9

Barber, Lynn 80

Barr, Nikki 29, 36

Beckett, Andy 93, 170–1

Bernstein, Carl 182

Blair, Tony 118, 120–1, 167

Blanchflower, David 119–20

Bleasdale, Alan 179

Blunkett, David 121

Bly, Nellie 92–3

Boshoff, Alison 72

Bowie, David 109–10, 113

Brown, Gordon 117, 120–1, 123

Buckley, Samuel 15

Burgess, Anthony 104–5

Bush, Kate 72

Byrnes, Sholto 181–3

Capote, Truman 85, 88, 209

Cartarescu, Mircea 108

Chavez, Hugo 77

Chesterton, G.K. 9

Clegg, Nick 116

Cobbett, William 14

Cocozza, Paula 47, 53

Connolly, Cyril 13, 87, 208–9

Conrad, Joseph 100

Coveney, Michael 179

Cunningham, Michael 80–1

Curtis, Polly 139–40

Dargis, Manohla 113

Davidson, Andy 164–5

Defoe, Daniel 15, 99

Deng, Wendi 198

Dickens, Charles 9, 97, 199

Donnelly, Declan 41

Doughty, Kenny, 179

Douglas, Sarah 71

Emin, Tracey 175–6

Evans, Harold 31–2, 209

Fawkes, Guido, *see* Staines, Paul

Al-Fayed, Mohamed 31, 38

Fielding, Henry 15

Finnigan, Judy 178

Fisk, Robert 91, 174–5

Flanders, Stephanie 60

Foden, Giles 100

Foot, Paul 91

Freedland, Jonathan 156

Gagosian, Larry 70–1

Galloway, George 77

Gellhorn, Martha 194–6, 209

Gillan, Crawford 31

Goldenberg, Suzanne 82–4

Gowers, Sir Ernest Arthur 42

Grayling, A.C. 101–2
Greene, Graham 9, 85, 97–8
Greer, Germaine 177
Greer, Ian 38
Hall, Macer 34
Hamilton, Neil 31, 38
Hansard, Thomas 'T.C.' 14
Harding Davis, Richard 84–5
Harris, John 158–9
Hartley, L.P. 171
Harvey, Fiona 35
Hattenstone, Simon 56–8
Hattersley, Roy 119
Hearst, William Randolph 84
Hemingway, Ernest 9, 85–8, 133
Hersh, Seymour 84, 93–4
Heseltine, Michael 166
Hislop, Ian 15
Hoggart, Richard 98–101
Hopkins, Katie 120
Huddlestone, Tom 112
Hundal, Sunny 136–7
Huxley, Aldous 97
Ishiguro, Kazuo 111–3
Jackson, Michael 28–30, 35–6
Jacobson, Howard 119
Jenkins, Simon 119, 121
Johnson, Boris 119
Johnson, Samuel 102
Jones, Owen 119, 133
Kelly, Lorraine 178
Kerouac, Jack 10, 85
Kerridge, Jake 69
Kesey, Ken 10, 90
Khan, Imran 60–2
bin Laden, Osama 174–5
Lansbury, Angela 69–70
Lea, Andy 63
Lee, Laurie 97
Lippmann, Walter 25
Littlejohn, Richard 120–1, 178
Littlewood, Joan 109
LoBianco, Lorraine 70
Lydon, John 193–4

McBride, Damian 123
McCaffrey, Darren 40
McCormack, Kirsty 192
Macdonald, Dwight 91
McEwan, Ian 68–9
McGrath, Melanie 175–6
McKeating, Justin 124–5
McPartlin, Anthony 41
Madeley, Richard 178
Mandelson, Peter 167
Major, John 167
Marr, Andrew 170
Mars-Jones, Adam 80–1
Maugham, W. Somerset 97
Moir, Jan 119
Monbiot, George 121
Moore, Suzanne 177
Moran, Caitlin 187–8
Moreton, Cole 53–4, 93, 152–4
Murdoch, Rupert 198
O'Carroll, Brendan 192
Orr, Deborah 177
Orwell, George 9, 42, 85–7, 97, 105, 133, 160–1
Paine, Thomas 14
Paul, Aaron 62–3
Perry, Andrew 193–4
Petridis, Alexis 110
Phillips, David 124–5
Phillips, Melanie 178
Pilger, John 92
Plaber, Alan 179
Prescott, John 122
Pulitzer, Joseph 16, 92
Randall, David 198
Reed, Lou 56–9
Robey, Tim 112
Romanek, Mark 112–3
Ronson, Jon 164–6
Roosevelt, Theodore 92
Ross, Jonathan 178
Russell, Willy 179
Russell, William Charles 84
Savile, Jimmy 78–9

Self, Will 9
Sergeant, John 166
Sewell, Brian 178
Simpson, Paul 73
Sinclair, Iain 100
Smith, Tim 31, 38
Snow, Jon 133
Staines, Paul (aka Fawkes, Guido) 123
Straw, Jack 121
Swift, Jonathan 15
Thatcher, Margaret 74–8, 159–60, 167
Thompson, Hunter S. 10, 85, 89–91, 209
Thornton, Sarah 80
Tomalin, Nicholas 208
Tonkin, Boyd 108
Toynbee, Polly 121

Twain, Mark 181
Tynan, Kenneth 109
Unwin, Stephen 110
Wade, Alex 76
Walker, Peter 35
Warhol, Andy 57, 103
Waterhouse, Keith 196, 210
Welles, Orson 84
Wells, H.G. 96–7, 209
Wenger, Arsene 73
Wilde, Oscar 208–9
Wilkes, John 15
Wodehouse, P.G. 9
Wolfe, Tom 10, 85, 90–1, 197
Woodward, Bob 182
Woolf, Virginia 68
Young, Hugo 74–5

GENERAL INDEX

active sentences, 151–3, 158
active writing, 149–67, 172
adjectives, use of, 42, 86–9, 152–7, 168–70
adverbs, use of, 88, 152–7, 168–9
angle, 7, 33–5, 39–41, 49, 51, 108–9, 138, 150, 162, 189, 210

blogs:
    comment-based, 103, 122–5, 136
    live, 122, 129–34

captions, 27, 128, 207
clichés, avoiding, 9, 13, 34, 143, 185, 196–7
circular feature/review, 50–4, 75, 113
collaborative reporting, 11, 125, 129, 135, 139–41
colour writing, 40, 43–5, 56, 82, 84–5, 88, 105, 169–73, 186, 197
columns, 95, 99, 103, 107, 114–5, 120–1, 173, 177–8
comment pieces, 9, 11, 100, 114–5, 119, 128, 133, 173, 197
comment, avoiding, 56, 84
consumer piece, 43, 63–4, 104
content-writing, 141–5
copy-writing, 141–5
criticism (see critics; reviews)

critics, 13, 80, 87, 91, 95–6, 103–14, 130–1, 133, 178–9
crowd-sourcing, 137–41
cutting, 203, 205–6

discussion-threads, 129, 135, 142

editing, 203–7
essays:
    journalistic, 95–102
    for specialist audiences, 101–2
experiential writing, 63, 89, 91, 104, 176
e-zine, 23, 210

Facebook, 11, 48, 132–5, 142
features:
    how-to, 63–4
    interview-based, 54–63
    issue-based, 43–54
    news backgrounder, 43–54, 80, 198
    tried-and-tested features, 63–4
first person, use of, 10–11, 57–8, 63, 73, 85, 89–90, 104, 106, 110, 139, 173–9
five Ws, 23, 25–8, 35, 39, 106, 150, 162, 168
frame and fill, 46, 52
framing, 67–8, 69, 109–10, 117, 150, 157, 167, 172

gatekeeping, 24, 130

hagiography, avoiding, 15, 79
Hansard, 14
hatchet job, 79–81
headlines, 23, 27, 41, 73, 128, 131, 134, 196–7, 207
hits (*see* page impressions)
house style, 109, 199–202, 207
hyperlink, 135–7, 146
humour, use of, 123, 197–8

infotainment, 98
interviewing, 11, 43, 50, 54–63, 93–4, 144, 169–70, 173–5, 187, 190–3
intros:
    delayed drop, 39–40, 159, 182
    dropped, 40–1, 68, 82, 97, 125, 156, 158–9, 198
    straight, 34, 40, 158
    twenty-five word, 27–33, 36, 157

jargon, 42, 142–3, 201, 208
journalism:
    digital/online, 9, 11, 14, 23–4, 27, 30, 44, 98, 100, 104, 122, 125–29, 131–43, 157, 164, 185–6, 201, 203, 207, 210–1
    citizen, 14, 43, 122, 127–32, 136
    confessional, 177
    gonzo, 10, 85, 88–91
    hyper-local, 125
    investigative, 16, 43, 85–94, 124, 137
    literary, 80, 85–94
    new, 10, 85, 88–91
    origins, 9, 13–6
    print, 11, 15, 23–4, 27, 30, 44, 104, 126–35, 164, 185–6, 200–1, 204, 207, 211

leaders, 103–4, 114–19
lineage, 204

magazines, 9, 15, 43–4, 63, 73, 74, 99, 101, 104, 114, 119, 128, 132, 134, 151, 176–7, 200–1, 204, 207, 211
    consumer, 76, 101, 115
    lifestyle, 126
    specialist, 73, 75, 105
    trade, 10, 210

news agency, 10, 93
news break, 35–9
news construction, 25, 158
news in brief (NIB), 33
news selection, 25
news:
    hard, 27–39, 82
    human interest, 16, 40–1
news-gathering, 25, 82, 138, 211
news-wire, 38–9
newspapers, 9–10, 15–6, 23, 30, 33, 40, 43, 60, 63, 66, 69, 73, 96–7, 99, 104–5, 111, 114, 118–19, 128, 131–2, 134, 149, 151–2, 177, 185, 200–4, 207, 209, 211–12
nutshell paragraph (nut-graph), 49–51
nouns, use of, 31, 87, 152, 155, 168–9, 171

obituaries, 65, 76–80, 95
op-ed, 103–4, 114–5, 119–20
opinions (*see* blogs; columns; critics; leaders; op-ed; reviews)
outro, 46

page impressions, 24
page-views, 164
pamphleteer, 9, 13, 15
paragraphing, 161–7
passive writing, avoiding, 149–67, 201
past tense, use of, 180, 184–8, 196
pay-off line, 77
peg, 70, 76, 99, 101, 106, 108, 139, 177
people first, 33–5
plain English, 41–3, 100, 201–2

polemic, 9, 14, 121, 125
present tense, use of, 55, 82, 180, 184–8
prioritizing information, 157–8
profiles, 11, 43, 65–81, 96–7, 158
propaganda, 14
proper nouns, 200–1
proofreading, 207
public relations (PR), 127, 142, 144, 190
Pulitzer Prize, the, 80, 92, 182
punchline, 40–1, 47, 49, 97, 110, 140, 150, 156, 165, 183, 199
puns, 196–7

Q&As, 43, 55, 58–63
quotes:
    direct, 35, 65, 175, 188–96
    indirect, 180, 188–91, 193
    verbatim, 55–6, 191, 193, 196

really simple syndication (RSS), 24
repetition, avoiding, 42, 143, 169, 191
reportage:
    campaigning/crusading, 91–4, 124
    investigative, 28, 85–8, 91, 93–4
reported speech (see quotes, indirect)
reviews, 11, 64, 66, 80, 96, 103–14, 128, 130, 173, 176, 178–9, 197, 209

semi-colons, avoiding, 198–9
sequencing, 50, 55, 86, 150–1, 157–8, 160–4, 166, 172
showing, 11, 51, 55–7, 59, 63, 67–8, 86–7, 89, 105, 151, 166, 170
signposting, 137, 161–7, 190
social media, 14, 122, 125, 130, 135, 141–2, 169, 210
sources, use of, 44, 50, 65–6, 128, 137, 170
spoilers, avoiding, 107, 111–3

storyboarding, 51, 164
structure:
    burger/sandwich, 106–11
    diamond, 134, 137
    inverted pyramid/triangle, 24–6, 50, 106, 134, 137, 162
    journey, 51–2, 56
    sentence, 153, 157–61, 180–2
style guide, 200–2
subbing, 26, 128, 196, 199, 204, 207
syntax, 42, 157

tautology, avoiding, 29, 191, 205
teaser, 37, 40, 68, 97, 110–1, 159, 164, 182–4
three-dimensional storytelling, 45, 55, 58, 67, 134–5
Tumblr, 125
tweeting, 24, 27, 122, 126, 129–34, 140, 209
Twitter, 11, 27, 73, 125, 132–5, 142

user-generated content (UGC), 135, 138

verbs, use of, 11, 31, 42, 87, 152–7, 168–9, 171
views-papers, 119–22
visitors, 142
visual writing, 32, 58, 130, 134, 156, 163, 168–72, 180

wasted words, 205
weblogs (see blogs)
who, what, where, when, why, how (see five W's)
word count, 25, 27, 64, 203–6
wordplay, 197
write-through interviews, 55–8, 62, 64